A Little Book of Leadership Lessons

Steph Edusei

First published in the UK in 2025 by Moja Publishing.

MOJA PUBLISHING

www.thisismoja.com

Praise

‘Finally, a leadership book that feels like a great novel! Insightful, engaging, and refreshingly concise.’

Claire Bennett, Regional Director, Common Purpose

‘A must-read for aspiring and experienced leaders alike. Packed with real-life lessons, not jargon, this book is an authentic and invaluable guide to leadership.’

James Carss, Diversity and Inclusion Champion, Founder and CEO, Castle Peak Group

Dedication

To my Mam, who has always led with love, strength, and quiet determination. Your example has shaped the leader and person I am today, and for that, I am endlessly grateful.

And to my daughter, Yasmin – you are my greatest inspiration. May you always know that you are enough, exactly as you are, and may you lead your own journey with confidence, humour, kindness, and joy.

I love you to the moon and back!

Contents

Introduction

Welcome to A Little Book of Leadership Lessons. When I decided to write this book, I knew straight away that it would be a little book. Not 'little' in that it was diminished or insignificant, but 'little' in that it is, I believe, short and snappy. I want it to be the type of book that people will pick up and think, 'This doesn't look too overwhelming to read.' I want it to be the type of book you can dip in and out of and get something out of every chapter individually, without having to read the whole thing. If I'm honest, I want every chapter to be the type of thing you can read on the loo when you are grabbing a few minutes' peace and quiet. I hope it feels like you're sitting down having a chat with me over a cuppa, something I always love to do. I don't want my book to add any stress or obligation to your life, because that's what I intend it to help release you from.

I do a fair bit of speaking at events and conferences, and always get some really beautiful feedback about how my words have resonated with others' experiences, and how I've made people think about their lives and practices. Sometimes I bump into people months or even years later, or they seek me out, and they tell me how my words have stayed with them and what they've done as a result. I'm honoured and grateful to be in a position I can help people in this way. But I can only talk to a certain number of people at a time and, if I'm to do anything else with my life, I can only take on a certain number of public speaking events, and that limits how many people I can engage with. If you're anything like me, you'll hear a talk and find it really interesting and relatable but then forget a lot of the key information after a few days or weeks. So, writing a book seemed like a good thing to do.

I actually started to write this book – although to be honest it wouldn't have been *this* book – about six years ago. Life took over and I stopped writing and pretty much told myself that I wasn't going to be an author; it was one of those time-consuming things I didn't have time to do. That was probably fear speaking as much as anything else; I didn't want to commit, start, and stop again. But people kept telling me that I should write a book and, more importantly, that they'd love to read it. So, after hearing Susan Routledge talking about her 'little book' on the *Beyond the Bio* podcast, I was inspired to start writing again and to write my own little book. In reality, the book was already written: it had been cooking in me for some time, and was ready to be put down in words.

People have asked what the book is about. Well, it's about leadership, of course, but more importantly it's a reflection on my leadership journey and some of the key lessons that I've learned from my many and varied experiences. Like anyone, I've had some challenges and setbacks in my life, but I've also had some wonderful opportunities and role models. In this book, I've tried to distil some of that into ten leadership lessons that I believe are helpful to others.

Which brings me to the second question I've been asked – who is the book for? Quite simply it's for anyone at any stage of leadership. I'd love new and aspiring leaders to read it and for it to help them if not avoid some of the situations, emotions and reactions I describe, then recognise them for what they are more quickly than I did, and understand and absorb the learning from them. I want established leaders to find some comfort and learning from the following chapters as I know that many of these experiences are common to a lot of us. I'd like this book to help them to be able to reflect on their leadership journey so that they can grow in confidence and skill. I'd also be over the moon if leaders, both new and established, found learning within these lessons that will help them to better understand the people they lead, so that they can develop truly inclusive and nurturing environments.

I'm deeply indebted to the people who have cast an eye over draft versions of this book. Their feedback has helped me to develop it so that it's not just something that I'd want to read, but that will hopefully be accessible and valuable for everyone. One aspect of this is the inclusion of some key learning points and suggestions for further learning at the end of each chapter. If you don't feel it's important to dig into theories and read around a subject right now then just ignore that bit, I completely understand. But for those of you that do, this element gives a signpost to some places where you can explore the themes raised in each chapter.

I have really loved writing *A Little Book of Leadership Lessons*. I have pushed myself to be as open and honest as I can be, which has been an emotional process at times. That has led to new levels of discovery and learning, all of which I've shared within this book, and that I know will allow me to grow further as a leader – the journey is never over.

I hope that this book gives you some assurance and reassurance.

I hope it supports you as you work things out.

I hope it makes you think and question.

I hope it helps.

Chapter One

What Is Leadership?

The one where I explore what leadership truly means, how it differs from management, and why trust, emotional intelligence, and team dynamics are at the heart of effective leadership.

Before we start to talk about leadership lessons, I thought it might make sense to talk about what leadership actually is. I remember many years ago, when I was a very junior NHS manager, some established and respected leader, whose name I can no longer remember, asked me what the difference was between leadership and management. I, crippled with self-doubt and awe, told him I didn't know, so he told me that management was about things and leadership was about people.

That's fine as far as it goes, but it's rather generic and lacks anything tangible to help an aspiring leader to be the best that they can be. So, I wanted to start by sharing what I have learned about leadership. This first bit is quite technical, so those who love theoretical models will enjoy it, but for those of us that aren't so keen, don't worry: this isn't a textbook, there are no exams at the end, it'll be over quickly, and you may find it interesting.

I grew up as a leader during the time of real heroic leaders. In the 2000s, NHS leadership landscape was heavily influenced by Daniel Goleman's six leadership styles:

Coercive (aka directive): demanding immediate compliance

Authoritative (aka visionary): mobilising towards a vision

Pacesetter: high-performance standards for self and others

Affiliative (aka collaborative): building emotional bonds

Democratic (aka participative): creating consensus

Coaching: developing people for the future.

David Nicholson, chief executive of the NHS from 2006–2014, introduced assessment of NHS senior leaders against these leadership styles. Perhaps not surprisingly, most came out as having a dominant pacesetter style. I say 'not surprisingly' because, at the time the assessments were done, we had been through many years of the Labour government's NHS Plan, which had a strong emphasis on striving to meet waiting-time targets; something a pacesetter style is ideally suited to. What NHS leadership focused on at the time was that their leaders used, at best, two dominant leadership styles, and these were usually a combination of pacesetter and either coercive or authoritative. Goleman suggested that no one style was better than the others, but that a genuinely great leader was able to flex their style to suit the situation and need. As a hospital director once told me, if you're a patient bleeding uncontrollably on an operating table, you don't want the surgeon leading the team to be consulting with colleagues to create consensus on the best course of action. You want someone who will tell people exactly what to do in a way that ensures they do it straight away (as long as they're right, that is).

Why am I even bothering to give you this little NHS history and leadership style theory lesson? Well, because I think it might be helpful for you to know that my early steps towards becoming a professional leader were set in this predominantly pacesetter environment. I was taught that leaders set extremely high standards and demonstrate those standards. I was bred professionally in an environment where JFDI (Just ****ing Do It) was an accepted leadership approach. I was formed in a culture which had the narrative that successful leaders were the ones who reached the goal and hit the target. And I didn't fit that pattern at all.

Don't get me wrong, I loved operational management. I loved its unexpectedness and variability. I thrived on its fire-fighting nature, especially within hospitals and the ambulance service. It was all about having to solve a problem – now. It was about getting involved and saving the situation. It called to the rescuer and the hero in me, and the adrenaline rush I used to get from it was intoxicating. However, I knew that if I wanted to progress and make a bigger difference, I had to move away from being so focused on the operational and day-to-day elements of management and move towards more strategic, longer-term leadership work.

One of the main challenges I faced when moving into more strategic work, and further up the leadership ladder, was that I struggled to describe exactly what I had achieved. The language moved from 'I' to 'we', and I felt guilty claiming that I had delivered something that was obviously a collective effort. After all, it was the clinical staff or the project manager who had actually done the work; I was just their boss.

Even now, I have days when all I do is speak with people, listen to what is going on for them, hear their ideas and solutions, suggest a few ideas of my own, and give them 'permission' to do what they already know they should do.

I was once in a committee meeting at St Oswald's Hospice[1] , where I am now the Chief Executive, and we were talking about the work that a couple of departments had been doing and their plans for the future. A trustee commented that the change in their work over the previous two years was significant, and was praising the heads of department for how they'd transformed their teams. I wholeheartedly agreed with this: the teams had been fantastic in adapting, reviewing and learning, which has been invaluable during and since the Covid pandemic. The trustee then said that they thought I should also take credit for my leadership, as it had helped to create a sea change in culture, and this could be seen in the departments' work. Really nice to hear? Yes?

The next day I was chatting at home about this and said how it was lovely praise to get, but that all I'd really done was shown an interest, got involved, and supported them to do what they knew needed to be done. And it was then that all of my leadership learning coalesced into this one concept.

1. St Oswald's Hospice is a large charitable children's and adults' hospice based in the north-east of England www.stoswaldsuk.org/

A leader's role is to create the environment that allows others to thrive.

That's it. That's all we need to do. Create environments that allow others to thrive. Simple?! Well, maybe not so simple, as a skilled leader has to be able to identify the different environments that suit different team members in different situations and be able to create what they need; but the concept is simple.

Let me take you back to the surgical example of a patient bleeding uncontrollably on the operating table: what environment was needed then to allow others to thrive? One that is in control, where people are clear about their roles and what to do, where what needs to happen is clearly communicated in a timely manner? If that's the case, then a lead surgeon taking charge, being very clear about actions and indicating that immediate compliance is required probably creates just that environment. Whereas this would be a terrible approach in a multidisciplinary service or product design meeting; it would create completely the wrong environment.

So, what does this mean for the question of what leadership actually is?

Well, firstly a leader is only a leader if they have followers.

> *'He who thinks he leads, but has no followers, is only taking a walk.'* ***John Maxwell, American leadership author and speaker***

It's extremely easy to declare yourself a business leader, thought leader, social leader, etc., and for that to lend you an air of credibility. A title is easy to gain but a title does not make a leader. If all you get is a title with no substance, people will not follow you, no matter how much authority that title brings. This doesn't mean that people should do as you say without questioning you, but that they are willing to trust you enough to allow you to influence, guide, and manage them, their actions and thoughts.

As Chief Executive of Healthwatch Newcastle and Healthwatch Gateshead, I had to exert influence with very little positional authority or power. We were a very small organisation, working alongside huge healthcare organisations and local authorities. We could make recommendations but had virtually no organisational authority to ensure they were enacted. The way I managed to influence those organisations and the individuals within them to change was through building trust.

Patrick Lencioni describes the kind of trust leaders and teams need as the type of trust that allows people to admit when they've made a mistake or they don't have the answers; that enables them to ask for guidance; to be honest with you; it allows them to be vulnerable and is the basis for building teams.

The way in which you gain that trust is, in most cases, through your actions. Yes, some people are great talkers, and we can all point to notable exceptions to the 'actions speak louder than words' rule: leaders who are fabulous at self-promoting but who don't actually do what they say they will or who act in a way that opposes what they talk about. However, despite appearances, most people aren't either skilled or brazen enough to achieve that. Our actions usually show through despite what we say, so the way in which we conduct ourselves in all situations is important for us to establish trust and a bond with our potential followers. Your thoughts, words, and deeds have to be in alignment, or people will see that your claims are hollow.

I have to add here that we are not either leaders or followers. It is possible and, I think necessary, to be both. Different times and situations will dictate the role that we play. Even though I'm a leader in many situations, there are still many people I'm happy to follow and defer to when needed.

Second, a leader isn't any one thing or one type of person. If you ask most people to describe a leader, they will probably talk about someone very charismatic, strong, assertive, passionate, decisive, and, overwhelmingly, male (don't believe me? Just Google the word 'leader' and see the words and images it comes up with).

Being a charismatic leader is absolutely what is needed... in some situations. The same can be said for all of the other adjectives. At times as a leader you will need to be all of those things but, thinking back to Goleman's leadership styles, it's vital that we are competent in all six styles. We have to be able to decide which style suits an individual or a situation and use them appropriately. The best leaders have a control panel full of skills, styles and traits: they know when to turn up the dials on the ones that are needed and when to dial others right down.

> *'A leader is best when people barely know he exists. When his work is done, his aim fulfilled, they will say: we did it ourselves.'* ***Lao Tzu***

Third, leaders are often very competent individuals. Many of us can do many things and professionally many of us have done the roles of the people we lead. Despite this, great leaders usually don't do: they show, they guide, they give space. I often joke that I have the easiest job in the hospice because I'm surrounded by great people who know their thing. They come and discuss their thing with me, tell me what we should be doing, and then I say, 'Great! Do that, then.' Now, of course, I am joking; my job is a little bit more involved than that. But quite often, leadership is knowing when to get out of the way. I am full of ideas, dreams, and passion, but not all of it is right, most of it is not right now, and it's not about me anyway. When, as leaders, we bring together our skills, styles, and traits in the right combination to create an optimum environment, our teams should absolutely believe that they achieved things themselves, because they did.

We should also be careful about needing that recognition. Leaders walk a delicate line between being the person people look to and the person people see; between accepting credit where it's due and ensuring that others get the credit they deserve. Being recognised is extremely intoxicating, and it's easy to succumb to flattery and recognition. But in the same way that we need to recognise that we only lead if people see something they want to follow, leaders need to understand that we only achieve because others support us to do so. No matter how intelligent, creative, inspirational, entrepreneurial, or accomplished we are, we are reliant on others in other parts of our companies, organisations, or lives who enable us to succeed. A little humility and appreciation of this goes a long way in cementing that trust and bond I mentioned earlier. I also believe that it helps to develop other leaders: showing that you are not superhuman with limitless skills, energy, and acumen allows others to recognise their own worth and see their perceived weaknesses as elements of just what they are, part of being human, not a barrier to success.

There is far more to being a leader than I have talked about here. I've tried to describe some of the things that, in my experience, leaders can do to create the right environment for teams to thrive. I hope that the coming chapters will show you some of the lessons I have learned, drawn from my experience, and will help you to avoid some of the mistakes I've made, and allow you to be kind to yourself when you inevitably make mistakes of your own.

Key Learning Points

Leadership vs. Management: Leadership is about people, while management focuses on systems and processes. Leadership inspires, motivates, and builds trust; management organises, plans, and executes.

The Trust Equation: Trust is foundational to leadership. It is built through credibility, reliability, intimacy, and self-orientation. Leaders who focus less on themselves and more on others create stronger, lasting bonds with their teams.

The Evolution of Leadership Understanding: Leadership is not static; it evolves with experience and self-awareness. Leadership often involves uncertainty, but growth comes through reflection and learning.

Effective Team Dynamics: Great leaders understand that developing collaboration and resolving conflict are critical to building high-performing teams.

The Role of Self-Reflection: Leadership is a journey of constant self-improvement. Effective leaders actively seek feedback, reflect on their actions, and commit to personal growth.

If you want to learn more take a look at:

Charles H Green's *The Trust Equation,* first referenced in *The Trusted Advisor* by David H Maister, Charles H Green and Robert M Galford (Book)

Patrick Lencioni's *The Five Dysfunctions of a Team.* (Book)

Simon Sinek's *Leaders Eat Last.* (Book)

Chapter Two

You Are Enough

The one where I confront imposter phenomenon, share how it shaped my life, and outline the steps I took to reclaim my confidence and recognise that I am, and always have been, enough.

I have experienced imposter phenomenon for most of my life. I allowed it to influence pretty much every decision I made, big or small, for many years. I often talk about a photograph I have of me on a Brownie holiday. I'm about eight years old, I have an apron tied around my waist and I'm performing a ballet dance called the Breton Fisherman's Dance in front of everyone there. I look at that photo and think about the girl I was then. As a mixed-heritage girl growing up in Newcastle upon Tyne in the 1970s, I knew that I was different, but at that age I can't recall being particularly worried about not belonging. I had good, close friendships; I had a loving, supportive family; I had dancing and Brownies: all places where I belonged.

Fast forward just a few years to when I was about twelve and all of this had changed. I still had friendships, the family, dancing and

Guiding, but the way I felt was different. I felt like I didn't belong in most situations. I felt like people were tolerating my presence rather than welcoming it, and I believed I wasn't enough. At twelve.

This continued throughout my teenage years. It followed me into young adulthood, and was there when I was a mother, a leader, and a coach. It didn't just remain, though: it grew. It fed off my natural teenage insecurities, it was nourished by my young adult relationships and experiences, it thrived on the uncertainties that come when you are a parent, leading your first team, supporting others. I permitted imposter phenomena to inform and craft my life.

As a young person, I wanted to be a performer, a triple threat: an actor, singer, and dancer. But by my mid-teens, I was telling myself why I wasn't going to make it. At the time, there were very few successful Black actors, and the female Black actors who made it were all tall, slim, and gorgeous.

At 5 ft 5, I wasn't tall. At 8½ stone (119 lb), I was described as a 'big girl' at dancing, and I certainly wasn't sought out by the good-looking lads at school, so I thought I was probably not gorgeous either. So, even though I went to university to study performance art, I didn't pursue my dream in a consistent, persistent way, and I dropped out after two years. I believed I wasn't a good enough performer and didn't look the right way to get to where I wanted to be.

Professionally, over the years, I let imposter phenomenon prevent me from applying for jobs, asking for help, saying that my workload was excessive, asking for more pay, taking credit for my work. I permitted it to push me to work excessive hours, to take on additional responsibilities without any recognition in terms of pay or seniority, to sacrifice time with family and friends, to push myself to the brink of depression and to illness: I actually had a brain haemorrhage. Yes, I was ill because I felt that I wasn't good enough and I was constantly afraid of being found out as an imposter.

In the summer of 2016, I was really stressed. I was running my own business alongside running a not-for-profit, parenting, dealing with a controlling and needy boyfriend, and a hundred other things. I had a few days off and came down with a mystery illness – I was vomiting and felt weak. This wasn't unusual for me as, because I worked on the edge all the time, whenever I stopped for a holiday I was hit by some form of illness. As usual, I recovered after a few days. A month later, I suddenly developed thunderclap headaches over a twenty-four-hour period, then kind of recovered. A week later, I was in hospital, having had a brain haemorrhage. It was caused when, as the Swiss cheese safety theory[1] would say, all the holes lined up. I'd had a viral infection, which in rare cases can lead to a condition where the blood vessels in the brain can constrict and, in rare cases, that can lead to a brain haemorrhage. I was one of those rare cases.

I was very fortunate and have little lasting damage from the haemorrhage, but the imposter phenomenon was still there and it told me that I couldn't let anyone think I was even less than I'd been before I had my brain haemorrhage. So I worked harder. I allowed myself to get so entangled with imposter phenomenon that I gave it control over huge parts of my life. Fast forward eight months, and I was privately crying all the time and on the brink of depression. It was at that point that I realised I had to tackle the imposter phenomenon.

---

1. The Swiss cheese model is a safety model of accident causation developed by Professor James Reason

Now, I'm sure you want me to tell you how I tackled it, and I will, but first I want to talk about imposter phenomenon and why I now don't call it imposter syndrome. For anyone who doesn't know, imposter 'syndrome' is probably most easily described as a persistent feeling of self-doubt and inadequacy. It usually includes the fear of being exposed as a fraud, regardless of one's success and accomplishments. There are many articles that link imposter 'syndrome' to things like neuroticism and low self-esteem, which can imply that there is something wrong with the person experiencing it. However, John Amaechi uses the term imposter phenomenon, pointing out that it is not an illness or a disease, and people who experience it are not broken. It is not a mental health condition, and not something you have to be cured of. And, despite what the internet would have you believe, I don't accept that it is a condition experienced by high-achieving individuals – or certainly not exclusively high-achieving individuals: my twelve-year-old self and a lot of young women will tell you that it can affect people at any stage of life and development.

Yes, I hear you saying, 'This is all really interesting, but how do I deal with imposter phenomenon?' So, this is how I learned how to control and manage mine. It didn't happen overnight and, as you'll see, some of it was personally challenging.

Notice

The first thing I had to do was to notice. I had to notice all the times that the voice I heard was talking. I had to notice how many times a day it popped up to tell me that I was not good enough, that I was wrong, that I was a fraud, or stupid, or too different. What I noticed was that in my case the voice was talking all the time. I often describe it as similar to working with music playing in the background. Often you will hear the music that's playing but not notice that the music is there, and then suddenly you find yourself singing along. The music was the voice and, without registering it, I'd begun to sing those self-critical lyrics.

Listen

The next step was emotionally tough. I had to listen. I had to listen to all the horrible, critical things the voice was saying to me, about me. And I noted them all down. Committed them to pen and paper so I couldn't hide from them. You can do this whatever way you want to. I used a notebook that I carried with me all the time, but you may want to make phone notes or pop them in a computer file. It really doesn't matter as long as it works for you, and you listen and write it all down. It's important not to filter this and to be as honest with yourself as possible, but it's also important to be kind to yourself. So don't do this before an event when you know you have to be at your best, and make sure you allow yourself space to feel the emotions that the words will bring up.

Look

What came next was perhaps the hardest step for me. I had to look for evidence that supported the things the voice had said about me. When you do this, you make yourself really vulnerable. Remember, if you have imposter phenomenon you already believe the things that you've noted down, so seeking out proof of them is terrifying and you believe that you will find it everywhere. Surprisingly, though, that evidence is usually more difficult to find than you think. In my case, it was pretty much non-existent.

Some of you may want to have someone who can sense-check things here, because if you experience imposter phenomenon it's easy to manufacture supporting evidence. Ask someone you trust and respect if you can run past them some of the 'evidence' you believe proves the negative things about you to check it is true. This is also helpful because you may have weaknesses in some areas, and you may find evidence to support that. But what person doesn't have weaknesses? This is completely normal, and if those areas are relevant to what you want to do and achieve then they are areas for growth and development, not a reason to beat yourself up or to write off all your achievements and skills.

Looking is a two-part step. After you have looked for the evidence that proves what the voice has been saying, you need to look for the counter evidence. Funnily enough, I found a lot of counter evidence when I was looking for proof. Professionally, I found that I'd been asked to take on more responsibility or undertake new roles, as well as compliments I've been given (but disregarded). I had results from exams and development programmes as well as compliments on work I'd completed. People had told me that they wanted me to be part of various working groups because they loved my approach and perspective. I was praised for my public speaking and for how well I could communicate an experience or perspective. There was a plethora of counter evidence that showed that the voice was wrong.

Even now, I keep adding to that evidence. In the early days, I carried another notebook in my handbag to note down evidence, but now I'm more likely to use an email folder or a Word file.

Relearn

Once I had gathered all the evidence that the voice was wrong, I had to relearn the truth about myself. I would frequently – and I mean frequently, multiple times a day – check my book of evidence. Every time the voice popped up, I would either physically or metaphorically reach for my evidence and teach myself that what it was saying was wrong. Again, the way you choose to do this might differ. You might be the type of person who likes affirmations. I created some and had them as the lock screen on my tablet so I saw them throughout the day. I did not look at myself in a mirror and recite them, as that's just not me, but if that appeals to you then do it. You may simply need to read and refer to the evidence, or you may want to use someone like a coach to help you acknowledge and accept the new truth. Whichever way you approach it, with effort and consistency, the voice will gradually become less frequent and quieter, as it has for me.

Some of you will be able to stop there. It will work as long as you put in the work. You will have to practise maintenance, recognise what your imposter phenomenon triggers are, and do the work before you go into one of those environments where you will be triggered, but that should be enough for some. But my imposter phenomenon was deeply rooted and it needed more to manage it.

Now, this may sound a bit strange – to be honest, it is a little strange – but I had to create a persona for the voice. This was because I struggled with the concept that it was my inner voice. If it was my inner voice, then it must be speaking the truth. Why would I lie to myself? So, I had to separate the voice from me.

I started by thinking: 'Where does the voice come from? Where do I hear it?' For me the voice sits just behind my right shoulder. Don't ask me why! That's just where it seems to come from. It pulls and holds me back, telling me not to get above myself.

My next thought was: 'What does it sound like?' The voice I heard was pinched, nasal, and whiny

I then imagined what it looked like, and it looked much like it sounded: pinched, nasal, and a murky green. It was spiky, angular, and sinister.

So, I had an image of the voice. For some of the people I have coached, their voice has a clear gender and we can give it a name. The voice I hear is genderless. Initially, I referred to it as My Creature.

I knew that if I continued with this sinister and quite evil Creature talking to me, it would continue to hold some power over me. I had to make it less overpowering and frightening. So, I took the character that I'd pictured and caricatured it. It became a cartoon-like version of itself: a figure of fun. The voice became higher pitched and whinier, the colour more lime green and the image less threatening. That made it far easier for me to ignore what it was saying and for me to muzzle it. In fact, some of the images I created in my mind were of the Creature wearing a muzzle or in a cage.

I always say that I haven't driven out imposter phenomenon but I have tamed it. Over time, there have been some interesting transitions. First, there was a subtle change in its name, from My Creature to The Creature. The Creature has also shrunk to a fraction of its original size as my control over it, and my confidence, have grown. In some circumstances, it's more likely to try to get out of its cage. In the past, in these circumstances I would have engaged with the Creature and allowed it to control my thoughts and actions. Now, at those times, or ahead of them if I know they are coming, I do some maintenance work, revisiting my evidence and picturing the caricature to make sure I keep the Creature at bay.

For many years, this was my view of imposter phenomenon, but I started to think about why this had happened to me so early in my life. I questioned why it seemed to be far more common among young women and girls than in men and boys, and why it was more prevalent among ethnically minoritised people. Then I started to read work by people who denied that imposter phenomenon was a thing and argued that it was just our reaction to a world that 'others' us, that highlights our differences and discriminates against us. I now recognise that, while some of that feeling of not being good enough and fear of new circumstances is quite possibly attributable to a natural nervousness of new environments and challenges, some of what is attributed to imposter phenomenon is, in fact, us picking up on very real signals and behaviours that surround us and tell us that we don't belong.

More recently, for a few years I felt as if I almost had a split personality. In most of my professional life I felt happy, confident and secure, but in one area I felt less competent, more insecure and that I didn't belong. Reflecting on this, I recognised that this was mainly caused by external cues and messages telling me I was wrong, that I was only there by the grace of others, and that I was an outsider.

The label of 'suffering from imposter syndrome' is often used as an accusation and a stick to beat us with. It is used to imply that we are somehow weaker and not fit for the environment we're operating in. If we have imposter 'syndrome', it's our fault and we need to 'cure' ourselves. It is used to make us believe that we are in the wrong, not that there is anything wrong with our environment. However, the environment we are in sometimes does not want us there. We are not delusional, or insecure. We do not need to 'get a grip'. We are perceptive and emotionally intelligent.

With this in mind, I now have a further step if the imposter phenomenon voice starts up.

Ask

First ask, 'Is this the voice or is this my intuition?' If it's the former, I need to do the work on addressing my perception and building my confidence and self-esteem to handle the situation. If it's the latter, I have some very different work to do – but I'm the right person to do it.

Key Learning Points

Imposter Phenomenon is Not a Syndrome: It is not a mental health condition or a personal flaw. Using the term 'phenomenon' rather than 'syndrome' removes the implication of illness or brokenness.

The Impact of Imposter Phenomenon: It can deeply influence personal and professional life, feeding on insecurities, societal pressures, and systemic discrimination, often leading to burnout or even serious health consequences.

Recognising and Addressing the Voice: Notice: Acknowledge the internal voice of self-doubt and criticism. Understand how pervasive it can be in daily life.
Listen: Identify the specific things this voice says by writing them down. Confronting these thoughts is emotionally challenging but essential.
Look: Seek evidence for and against these self-critical claims. Counter evidence often reveals the voice's inaccuracies.
Relearn: Regularly revisit the evidence and create affirmations or rituals to internalise a more accurate and positive self-perception.
Creating a Persona for the Voice: Visualising and caricaturing the critical inner voice can diminish its power and help in managing its influence.

The Role of Environment: Imposter phenomenon is not always internal; external cues, biases, and systemic 'othering' play a significant role in fostering feelings of inadequacy.

Distinguishing Intuition from the Voice: When self-doubt arises, ask whether it stems from imposter phenomenon or genuine intuition. Address them accordingly.

If you want to learn more take a look at:

John Amaechi's *Reframing Imposter Syndrome* on LinkedIn.

Dr. Jessamy Hibberd's *The Imposter Cure.* (Book)

Chapter Three

The Busy-ness Myth

The one where I debunk the myth that being busy equals success, share how to prioritise what truly matters, and explore practical ways to reclaim time and balance in life.

In 2018, a former boss and dear NHS colleague of mine, Julie Ross, died prematurely. She was only in her forties, a few years older than me, and had daughters younger than my own. She was, and remains, much missed, and I think about her and channel her energy regularly.

Her funeral, which she planned herself, was very well attended by many of her NHS and social care colleagues; it was a bit of a 'who's who' of the north-east health and social care scene. As I circulated at the wake afterwards and chatted with former colleagues, something struck me. Their language.

'How are you?' I'd ask. 'How are things?'

'Busy,' they'd reply. 'Manic.' 'Frantic.' 'Things are crazy.'

Their words were accompanied by a huge sigh. I was transported to a few years earlier when I too would have responded in the same way. This, I believe, is down to a few things:

1. A lot of our public, voluntary, and community sector is seriously understaffed and definitely undermanaged. We have too few people trying to do too much, so they *are* busy.

2. Imposter phenomenon. This will keep us busy, as we feel we have to say yes to everything and be involved in everything, because if we don't and we're not, people will find out that we're not good enough.

3. The busy-ness myth.

Now, I don't have a solution for the first point, and I have a whole chapter about the second (see Chapter 2), so I'd like to address the third point here.

The busy-ness myth

I used to think that a full diary, preferably with back-to-back and overlapping appointments, was a sign of success. It meant I was in demand, needed, and important (remember that imposter phenomenon!). The fact that I was always on the go, dashing from one thing to the next, was a marker of seniority and achievement. After all, when I was a clerk typist my diary was clear. Because of this belief, I'd put up with an overcrowded diary, full of meetings, and with no time for me to do things or think. My 'doing' was pushed into what was supposed to be my personal time, and I'd end up working in the evenings and at weekends. I'd usually only be able to tackle things that were happening in the next few weeks, because I didn't have the headspace to horizon scan and imagine other scenarios. Nevertheless, I wore my busy-ness like a badge of honour that denoted just how key my role was and how much in demand I was.

I know, and not just from my experience at my colleague's wake, that it's the same for so many leaders. #hustle247 exists as social media hashtag for a reason. So much of our media depicts top and aspiring executives as people too busy to stop and eat, working long hours and neglecting their families. That's because, for so many, this is reality. Too many of us buy in to a culture that tells us that success = busy-ness.

I can recall looking at the diaries of managers whom I didn't rate very highly, seeing lots of free space and thinking that confirmed my opinion of their ability. But at the same time, I was envious of their space. However, one of the things I learned when I was dealing with imposter phenomenon, and the associated mental vulnerability, was that the 'busy = success' equation was a myth. Yes, busy people can be very successful, but people who create space in their day to eat, reflect, imagine, relax, and move can be just as successful – if not more. It is so important to respect yourself and your work enough to ensure that you care for yourself. Giving yourself the gift of time is one of the most powerful things you can do. I recall the first time I saw an interview with multi-billionaires Warren Buffett and Bill Gates. Warren Buffett showed his near-empty (paper) diary and said we should protect our time, as it's the only thing we can't buy more of.

That hit home.

A full cup simply overflows if we put more into it, and we are no different. Our 'overflowing' is usually done in a time when we should be recharging, and it can lead to overwhelm and ill health.

It is easy to create busy-ness and the perception that we are very hard-working, important, and successful – you just have to say yes to everything and get yourself involved in a lot. What isn't so easy is becoming less busy. Here are some of the tactics I employ to help break my addiction to busy-ness.

1. Conquering FOMO

Aside from, and sometimes because of, imposter phenomenon, one of the reasons we keep saying yes to things is FOMO (fear of missing out). We worry that if we don't say yes, and if we don't get involved, then we'll miss out on an experience. Professionally, we may be concerned that this might damage our career prospects or our relationships with colleagues. If you feel FOMO and it is driving you to say yes, then you need to learn to take a pause and critically evaluate the real potential impact of saying no. You might find it helpful to ask yourself the following questions:

- Is this a major project or meeting that could realistically alter the course of your career?
- Does saying no now mean saying no forever?
- What will suffer or need to stop to give you sufficient time to participate? Is that less important than the thing you're about to say yes to?

- Are you really the best/right person to do this, or are you just a reliable person or someone that others think should be involved?
- Are you tempted to get involved because you worry that you won't be able to influence the issue if you don't? Are there other ways you can make sure that doesn't happen? Is it about keeping control?

Answering these questions should help you to establish if it's something you really have to do, something you really want to do, or something you are saying yes to because of FOMO.

If it's the latter, say no.

If it's any other reason and you're going to say yes, you need to decide what is going to take a back seat or be dumped to make space for this.

2. Make space

Not everything is equally important. Nothing is equally important to everyone. What I mean is that some of the things you do are more important than others. In the personal space, I suggest that things that support your physical and mental wellbeing, such as eating well, doing things that bring you joy, resting, sleeping, and connecting with people you love, are more important than anything else. In your professional life, parts of the work you do will be much more important than other parts. But important to whom?

Taking some time to look at your workload and figuring out what is important to you, to your organisation or company, and to your boss is time well spent. I suggest that you go through your to-do list, if you have one (I hope you don't), your objectives, and about a month to six weeks of your diary and note all the things you're doing. Then assess how important each is. When doing this, make sure you don't confuse 'urgent' with 'important'. 'Important' means that it has great value. To not do an important thing will have bad consequences for the person it's important to. 'Urgent' just means that it has to be done soon. There are lots of unimportant things that people make urgent – I'd argue that, unless your home looks like a hoarder has moved in, cleaning it before a friend comes to visit is not important, but many people make it urgent (and if it does look like a hoarder has moved in, a quick, urgent clean isn't going to make it any better). I recall when a colleague wanted to make improvements to our on-call system. Would the improvements have been good? Of course they would. Was the system functioning as it was? Yes, it was. Were there more urgent things for us to focus on? Absolutely! And yet this colleague decided that this was an urgent and important task for their focus and attention. I had to draw attention to all of the other truly important and urgent work that needed their skill and the on-call system improvements took a back seat.

The best-known way to assess importance vs urgency is the Eisenhower matrix (Figure 3.1) – a simple 2×2 matrix where urgency decreases along the horizontal matrix (X) and importance increases along the vertical matrix (Y). Give it a try. I've found it useful, and not just in a work setting.

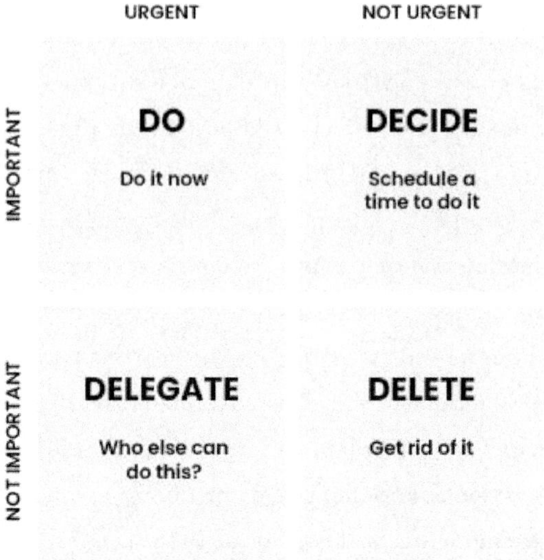

The Eisenhower matrix is often attributed to US President Dwight D. Eisenhower's attitude to work. It has since been popularised by various business writers including Stephen R. Covey in his book 'Seven Habits of Highly Successful People'.

I've also found it helpful to score things out of 6 on an importance scale. I chose 6 because it meant I had to make a judgement rather than taking the easy route and opting for the middle point of 3 out of 5 (an old trick I learned from my patient engagement work). The things you rate as 5 or 6, most important, are the ones you want to focus on.

However you decide to judge the importance of the work you have to do, it's important to discuss this with the people around you to check that you're not under- or overestimating its importance. Don't allow other people's opinion, or their desire to lighten their workload by adding things to your workload, to cloud your judgement, though.

Then, as the Eisenhower matrix above suggests, prioritise your work accordingly, even if the things in the 'Do' box are the things you hate doing and the things in the 'Delete' box are far more fun.

3. Does it have to be now?

If you ask me when something I want to happen needs to be done, I'll say 'now'. If you ask me when things that will take forward the organisation's objectives need to be done, I'll say 'now'. If you ask me when something that could safeguard and protect the organisation needs to be done, I'll say 'now'. All of this is important to me but it really isn't all urgent.

When we learn about objective-setting, we're told to set realistic timescales but I don't think enough time is spent discussing the 'realistic' part. What is realistic for me might not be realistic for you. I often tell my team: 'If I give you a timescale that is unrealistic, tell me. If we can't change it, let's have a conversation about what else can give.' Sometimes they remember, sometimes they go straight into delivery mode, and we only find that it's a problem when deadlines start getting missed or when people start getting really stressed.

So, my suggestion is to make sure that you have a conversation, with others or with yourself, about what are truly realistic timescales. Identify what else could be adjusted to accommodate new work or priorities: what can you delegate and what can wait?

4. Block out time

First of all, I have a confession: occasionally I have tried blocking out time for lunch or time for a walk during my working day. But what happens? I tend to ignore it and work through. I currently have half an hour each day designated as walking time and I'm yet to go for a walk! However, I haven't taken this time out of my diary, as it reminds me to move throughout the day and it's a promise to myself that I will go for a daily twenty-minute stroll… especially now I'm taking trainers to work as well as my heels (one step at a time). There are lots of things that get in the way of me taking the walk, for example lack of motivation or cold, wet weather, but time is rarely one of those things as I have that allocated. I'm still a massive advocate of diary blocking, even though the walk blocking hasn't worked for me… yet.

Some time ago, I was part of a fortnightly action learning set that ran for a few months. Once the set ended, the leader suggested we keep that time blocked out in our diaries to make space to think and read. I did just that. I have half a day per fortnight of focused work time. This time can be moved to accommodate other things, and I'll sometimes put 'action items' in my diary during the focused work time (more on action items in a minute), but it is rarely cancelled.

I also used to run a fortnightly radio show but gave that up because, while it was fun, I had other, more important things to do. The stress of trying to do it all and the feeling of letting people down gradually took away the benefits. However, when I gave it up, I left the time I had blocked out in my diary as 'keep free' time. This has been especially useful as it is a Friday afternoon, so an ideal time to tie up loose ends and reflect on the week. I've found these blocks of time give me exactly what they were supposed to do: space to read, space to connect with colleagues, space to think.

As I mentioned, I also like to use action items in my diary. These are appointments to complete work. For example, I might need to write a report for the Board or prepare a presentation. I'll decide how much time this will take me and make an appointment with myself to do the work. I include the deadline for the work in the title and, because this works for me visually, use a different colour for these appointments so I can clearly see they are action items. Of course, sometimes these get moved to accommodate other things or because I'm not in the right frame of mind for the task. Including the deadline means that I can do this easily, but this serves as a useful reminder of what has to be done, and a placeholder to free up time to do it.

5. Plan ahead

Sometimes I just get busy. There are times when everything colludes to fill up my work and social diaries and no amount of saying no, negotiating timescales, blocking out time, or other magical solutions will help.

Things will come out of nowhere to take up your capacity: all those meetings and events deferred from August (because no one wants to meet in August) will be pushed into September, or your child's school will announce an event that parents have to attend with ten days' notice when you already have a full week. It happens.

A little stress is good for you and we can cope with some periods of high stress: however, we can't function at that level all the time. We need downtime and troughs to counteract the peaks. It's all about balance.

The best way to find that balance is to plan ahead. Plan in some recuperation time.

September 2024 was a really full month for me, and weekends throughout September and October were busy with dance rehearsals ahead of a big show, so I booked in some days off to ensure that I wasn't working for fourteen days without a break. If you've got a busy fortnight, block out more time the fortnight afterwards to pick up things that have had to take a back seat – and this includes your self-care. Do not allow the busy-ness myth to make you think that you can't, or that doing this makes you less effective.

6. Trust your instincts

You know when you're too busy. You know when the work you're doing isn't important or valuable. You know when the timescale is unrealistic. You know when you're about to get overwhelmed.

Trust your instincts.

Once you've accepted that being busy is not an indication of worth or success, it is easier to put in place the right actions to free up your time and help you better manage your commitments and workload. But trusting yourself, and trusting your instincts, is key.

Key Learning Points

Busy-ness Does Not Equal Success: The notion that a full diary equates to importance and success is a myth. True success often involves creating space for reflection, relaxation, and thoughtful action.

The Cultural Trap of Busy-ness: Social norms and media glorify overworking and busy-ness, which can lead to burnout, reduced effectiveness, and compromised wellbeing.

Make Space for What Matters: Prioritise activities based on their importance rather than urgency, and focus on tasks that support physical and mental wellbeing.

Realistic Timelines and Delegation: Challenge unrealistic expectations, both from yourself and others, and don't hesitate to delegate or defer tasks when necessary.

Plan for Balance: Use tools and techniques to remove unnecessary work and help anticipate periods of busy-ness. Intentionally schedule downtime and recuperation to maintain long-term effectiveness and wellbeing.

Trust Your Instincts: Listen to your inner voice when it tells you you're overwhelmed or spending time on low-value activities.

If you want to learn more take a look at:

Bernard M. Bass and Ronald E. Riggio's *Transformational Leadership.* (Book)

Warren Buffett's advice on time management (available on YouTube).

Eisenhower Matrix templates for task prioritisation.

Forbes' *This Is Why Talking About How 'Hard' You Work Makes You Look Incompetent.* (Article)

Daniel Goleman's *Emotional Intelligence.* (Book)

Harvard Business Review's *Learn When to Say No.* (Article)

Harvard Business Review's *The Subtle Art of Saying No.* (Podcast)

Chapter Four

Surround Yourself

The one where I explore how the people and influences we surround ourselves with shape who we are, and share how curating positive relationships and environments can transform our wellbeing and growth.

> *'You are the average of the five people that we spend the most time with.'* ***Attributed to Jim Rohn, motivational speaker***

If this is true, then you need to pick those five people very wisely. In reality, while the phrase is snappy, probably a lot more than five people actually influence who you are, how you behave, and what you think. This is becoming more evident as the use of social media by political parties and other influences becomes better understood. What we consume, we believe, and what we believe influences our behaviour.

Just after my brain haemorrhage (if you haven't read the chapter on imposter phenomenon then this may come as news to you), I realised that I was carrying a lot of additional weight. I'd been overweight before the haemorrhage, and had then comfort eaten my way through a difficult relationship break-up. So, at the beginning of the year, I decided I needed to lose weight to make sure I stuck around to finish raising my daughter. She needed me. Of course I wanted to see her grow up and become an adult, but at the time my main drivers were other people's needs, and so it was the fact that she would be devastated if I died that made me determined to be healthier. I joined a weight-loss class and focused on it with the same dedication that I focused on work, and reached my target weight in about ten months. I felt brilliant! But that feeling was short lived, because I began to realise just how close to an emotional breakdown I was. I had focused on my physical health but ignored my mental wellbeing. When I look back on the years leading up to that time, I see that I had surrounded myself with some negative people and voices.

'Person' 1: Many years earlier, when I was on the NHS Management Training Scheme, the scheme leaders told us that we should be reading the broadsheet newspapers to ensure that we were well informed on current affairs and that would make us better NHS leaders. I told myself that I didn't have time to read the papers. I probably didn't, as I was intent on being busy all the time, but the next best thing was listening to the Radio 4 *Today* programme on the way to work each morning. That progressed to me listening to Radio 4 all the time when I was in the car.

For anyone who doesn't know, Radio 4 is a talk-only radio station provided by the BBC. It tends to be very middle-class in its output, and covers a huge range of topics from news and current affairs to nature and science, the arts, comedy, and the shipping forecast. I consumed an average of four to six hours of radio a day, and a large part of this was news and current affairs. I don't know if you've noticed, but the bulk of news programming is – and always has been – fairly negative. Happy events seldom make the news. Therefore, I was consuming large amounts of negative news content on a daily basis.

'Person' 2: At the time, my guilty pleasure was watching a certain TV soap opera. I would record the omnibus edition and watch it in bed on a Sunday morning before my daughter got up. I believed it helped me relax – escaping into a fantasy part of the UK full of rolling hills and sheep. However, soap operas are not renowned for their lack of drama, and often this is drawn from storylines that cause heartache and misery. So, once a week I was consuming a couple of hours of betrayal, hardship, and sorrow, with a sprinkling of humour and romance.

'Person' 3: I was working alongside NHS and social care colleagues. The public sector has always been a challenging place to work, and the NHS in particular is under a huge amount of public and governmental scrutiny. Funding cuts were biting across the public sector, and it was starting to show. Everyone was overworked and frustrated that the changes they wanted to make were impossible or extremely challenging. Add to this the impact of the government's austerity policy on many of the people we were working with – those with the least in our society, who needed the most support – and it created a prevailing atmosphere of conflict and fruitlessness. My working day often experienced a snowball effect: one person would start with a small trouble, worry, or woe, which would be added to by the people around them and start to gain momentum, picking up concerns along the way, and before you knew it you'd have a huge snowball of misery that would take up all the space.

'Person' 4: I had a colleague at work who I suspected was going through some emotional challenges. They had gone from being a very supportive and warm individual to someone who was highly critical of colleagues and circumstances. They sowed division and mistrust, encouraging others to doubt each other and fuelling arguments. The fun, welcoming environment that we'd created started to crumble and, as the boss, I was the person that everyone – quite rightly – ran to with their woes.

'Person' 5: After my relationship ended, we tried to maintain our friendship. There were lots of issues with that relationship that I won't go into here, apart from saying that his behaviours and mental state made him difficult to be around. It was my choice to end the relationship, and as a result, each of our post-break-up conversations became emotionally charged and sorrowful.

So, my 'five people' were actually more like five situations or experiences that I lived daily. I was surrounded by negativity, sorrow, and pessimism. I'll move on to what I did to address and remove some of those 'people' in a minute, but I'd also like to talk about some of the amazing people who I've been blessed to have in my life.

'Person' 1: One of my early roles in the NHS was as a medical secretary, and my line manager also managed the whole of the clinical directorate. Bev is an impressive woman. The directorate's senior staff was heavily male dominated and a large proportion of those men were surgeons – cardiothoracic surgeons. They quite literally held people's lives in their hands on a daily basis, and this certainly showed in some of their behaviours. And yet Bev managed them and their demands.

She also took an interest in the people who worked for her. She took the time to initiate discussions with me about my aspirations, supported me, and suggested ways for me to progress. She brought the NHS Graduate Management Training Scheme to my attention, and she supported my secondment into a more senior organisation-wide role, even when the consultant I was working for had been less than happy with my replacement.

I left that role and organisation, as did Bev, but we have stayed in contact over the years and she has acted as a formal – and informal – coach and mentor on many occasions. She supported me through making the decision to leave the NHS and chaired an organisation I led. Although the pandemic halted our semi-regular catch-ups, I still keep up with Bev, who is now retired, online, and know she is at the other end of a message if I need her. Bev's genuine interest in me, and care for me and what I do, along with her wealth of experience and knowledge, made her an amazing person to have in my life.

'Person' 2: I became a dance teacher and found an outlet for my creativity by good fortune. It all came about because I was going to sing in public for the first time in a very long time and was understandably nervous about it. So, I approached my daughter's dance and performing arts school about having a few lessons. I enjoyed the lessons so much that I continued them after my public appearance. One day I was chatting with my teacher, Mavis, about how much I'd enjoyed dance, and ballet in particular, when I was young. She said that she was teaching a lot of 'mature' dancers and that they were taking it seriously, doing exams, etc. I decided that I was going to be one of her mature dancers. A few years later I had taken two ballet exams and had started professional training and teaching classes.

Mavis is an inspiration. She is warm and nurturing and makes everyone want to work hard for her. While she wants all her pupils to strive for excellence, she recognises that everyone's 'excellent' will be different, and works to help them be the best they can be. Alongside this, she acts as a counsellor and confidante to pupils of all ages. As a teacher it's a great joy, and a frustration, to see how even the youngest of dancers will work extra hard when Aunty Mavis is in the studio because they want to impress her and make her happy. The passion and enthusiasm that Mavis brings to her work, even after many, many years of teaching, and the genuine love and care she has for the people she works with, make her a shining example of how to do life.

'Person' 3: If you ask most people (especially a woman) who inspires them, their mother will usually feature quite highly on the list. I am no different. My mother (Mam, since I'm from the north-east of England) is impressive. She brought up three children, ferrying us all to and from various groups and activities; fed and clothed us and made sure we had what we needed; worked at least one job, but often took on additional work to help with the household finances; volunteered with the parent–teacher association, the Scouting executive and Guiding fundraising groups; was an attentive daughter, sister, and wife; hosted many extended family members for long and short periods; and much more. Mam has always been the type of woman who, when she saw something that needed to be done, rather than waiting for someone else to do it, rolled up her sleeves and got on with it. She's started and runs a charity, been a Brownie Guider and is still involved in Girlguiding, and is a powerhouse. She's also very nurturing and is always there for her children, grandchildren, and great-grandchild. Since I've become an adult my mam has increasingly become one of the few people I can go to when I have a problem, who I want to call when I've had a success, and who I laugh until I cry with. I know she's there for me, with love.

'Person' 4: Almost a year before I recognised the need to improve my mental wellbeing, I stumbled across an incredible community of women. I was dipping my toe into networking groups and, since I was focusing on coaching women at the time and felt more comfortable at women-led networking events, I booked a half-day networking session: there was nothing unusual about that. However, the session itself was far from ordinary. It was a supportive group that recognised and celebrated its members' successes, met people where they were, and encouraged them to do things that brought them joy. It was a group in which self-care was prioritised and seen as the root of our strength. At the end of the first session, I can remember saying that it wasn't what I was looking for, but it was exactly what I needed. I continued to be part of that group over the next few years, as it evolved and changed. We stayed connected with, and supportive of, each other throughout the Covid pandemic and, even though we no longer meet as a group, we still stay in touch online, celebrate successes, and encourage each other when we face challenges. We have laughed together, a lot, and cried together, and I feel blessed to have them in my life.

'Person' 5: Most people who have heard me speak will know that I love Maya Angelou. I'm ashamed to say that until about ten years ago, I didn't know that much about her. I'd read a couple of quotes by her that I really liked and vaguely knew that she was a writer and civil rights campaigner, but that was about it. It wasn't until I heard an audio version of her first autobiography, *I Know Why the Caged Bird Sings*, that I started to understand a fraction of who and what she was. There are lots of reasons why Maya Angelou is such an influential figure for me. I am in awe of how she lived life on her terms and refused to be bowed by her experiences. I am inspired by her fight for equality and justice. I am schooled by her ability to communicate, especially when her message was confrontational and challenging. I am astounded by the impact she continues to have, years after her death.

One of the things I love about Maya is that, in her writing and speech, she managed to provide such wonderful quotes for life. My two favourites are:

> *'I've learned that people will forget what you said, people will forget what you did, but people will never forget how you made them feel.'*

This has been a guiding perspective for me for many years now, particularly when it comes to aligning my words with my actions and the impact they have. I also love:

> *'Do the best you can until you know better. Then when you know better, do better.'*

None of us are perfect. I know I have made, and will continue to make, many mistakes. However, I strive to ensure that, once I know something is wrong, I improve and, if I can, I put right the errors that my lack of awareness or knowledge have created. This leads me on to my next observation.

Beware of pedestals

It happens so easily. We learn a little about someone and think they are great. We learn a bit more, and that reinforces that greatness. We may meet them – still great. We see they've done or achieved something – wow, they're amazing! It's so simple to look for the things we want to see, and that reinforces our perception of the person. Plus, often all we see or hear about a person is what they want to share, and we all want to portray ourselves in the best possible light. We can put people on pedestals and then, when they fall, and they often do, they fall a long way. At best we feel foolish, and in worse cases we can become resentful, untrusting, and cynical. I have fallen foul of this on a number of occasions.

Back in the days when I thought that I wanted my future to lie in the upper echelons of NHS leadership, there was a NHS leader who inspired me. Female, of mixed ethnic heritage and successful, Paula Vasco-Knight appeared to be everything I wanted to be. She ran a hospital trust and was appointed by NHS England as National Lead for Equalities. She had received a CBE in recognition of her work and achievements, and featured regularly in the *Health Service Journal*, the trade magazine for the NHS. I decided that I had to meet Vasco-Knight and, ideally, work with her. After all, if I could include her in the group of people I was surrounded by, just think what I could absorb! As pedestals go, I probably put her on the fourth plinth in Trafalgar Square.

However, in 2014, six years into her CEO role, news broke that the trust had suspended Vasco-Knight after an employment tribunal had criticised her treatment of two whistle-blowers. This started a catalogue of revelations. The whistle-blowers had raised concerns about Vasco-Knight's nepotism, and she resigned from her CEO role; in 2016 she was suspended from an interim CEO role at another trust for 'financial allegations' relating to a previous employer; in 2017 she was found guilty of fraud after diverting NHS funds to her husband. As falls go, it was spectacular and devastating.

It horrified me. This was the person I aspired to be. I had looked up to and admired her from afar, supported her public words and actions and, as I say, elevated her to hero status. I couldn't comprehend how someone could appear so right yet be so wrong. I had been naive and impressionable.

A less shocking but no less impactful incident happened with someone I respect and value to this day. Again, this was a person who had achieved so much of what I wanted to achieve, and who I saw as a role model. In terms of people leadership, I thought they could do no wrong. I was talking to them about work one day and about how I felt out of control and uncertain at times, and they shared an observation that stuck with me. They said that I seemed so calm and self-possessed all the time, that I reassured my team that everything was going to be OK. So, if the team was to ever see me anxious or uncertain, it could destabilise them and make them panic. This was in the days when I still allowed imposter phenomenon to drive my thoughts and actions. I took that observation and interpreted it as a need not to show vulnerability and to always present myself as in control.

A few years later, after I had learned to manage my imposter phenomenon, I recognised this comment for what it was: ill-judged in who it was delivered to and fundamentally incorrect. I now believe that sharing how you feel about a situation with your team can be done responsibly, without sowing unnecessary fear and panic, and that authenticity is vital. I have direct experience of how sharing some of the challenges I went through with mental health and imposter phenomenon have helped others. As a result, the halo I had placed on this person's head evaporated. As a recovering perfectionist, I now recognise that no one is perfect and therefore everyone makes mistakes. I know there is as much to learn from mistakes – other people's and our own – as there is from successes. I also try to make sure that I share my own imperfections with others. I share my doubts and my mistakes, my lack of knowledge in some situations and my annoying idiosyncrasies, all in an attempt to help people to see that imperfection is human and it doesn't mean that you can't achieve great things.

I've also come to realise that some people are not meant to be in your life forever, nor are they meant to be a beacon of all that is right. I have had people in my life who have been just what I needed at that time. I'm honoured to have been able to learn from them and draw from them the positive elements they were meant to deliver. And I know, because no one is perfect, that the positives will also be accompanied by negatives and flaws, but that doesn't detract from their value.

Getting your 'people' right

I did promise that I'd explain how I modified my surroundings so that I had the right 'people' there, and I'll do this now.

I did a news detox. I had become a news junkie, consuming news every chance I got and being malnourished by the content. So I decided to go cold turkey and stop listening to, watching, or reading the news. To help with this, I sought out positive, inspiring podcasts and put together uplifting playlists that I could listen to in place of news programmes. I was initially concerned that I'd lose contact with what was going on in the world, but I soon found that social media had that covered, as people would usually post when something important was happening. At first, I decided not to read these posts when I saw them, but just to acknowledge that something had happened and, if I wanted, I could ask someone I trusted about it. To do otherwise would have dragged me back into that world of negativity. I don't believe that I missed any significant events or that my ability as a human or as a leader was diminished as a result. I simply became happier.

My detox actually lasted for years. Even now, I rarely watch or listen to the news, and I don't read a newspaper. I will look up news items when I hear about them, going to reliable and trusted sources online so that I can be informed, but I don't spend time scrolling the internet for news.

I no longer watch soap operas. In fact, I don't watch a great deal of television. When I do, I tend to opt for programmes that are escapist and easy to watch; I need downtime and don't want to spend that taxing my brain or consuming fear and misery. Now, I acknowledge that this is very much my personal choice. Some people love dark content and it gives them the same sense of escape that I get from lighter viewing, but give me a Christmas film and I'm happy (and no, *Die Hard* does not count, and nor does *Gremlins*).

I have found a working environment that suits me and my values. We still have challenges, including funding and capacity issues, and I'm still operating in the same health and social care system, but the people I work with and our focus on what we do, and why, is a stark contrast to what I used to experience. 'Supportive', 'caring', 'innovative', 'compassionate', 'authentic', and 'fun' are just a few of the words I'd use to describe the team and environment at St Oswald's Hospice, and it's a delight and honour to lead them.

I had to make some tough decisions and allow myself to let some people go from my life. Change starts with you. You cannot make other people change. You can support them. You can role model ways of being and behaving. You can guide and mentor them. You cannot change them.

Communicating with people about how you receive them and the impact they have on you can be incredibly difficult and painful – and it may not be well received. However, when delivered with compassion and clarity, that honesty is a gift that they can choose to receive or reject. They can reflect on it and decide if they want to change anything as a result. They may not be ready to hear it, and may come back to you at another time. They may not be ready to change. But even if they do hear you, whether or not they choose to act on your feedback is their choice. How you experience them is not necessarily going to be significant to them. You can't make people change.

While you can't make people change, you *can* change who you surround yourself with, and sometimes that's what you have to do.

So, while we may be more than just 'the average of the five people we spend the most time with', we are definitely informed, fed, and moulded by the thoughts, words, and actions of the people we interact with frequently. Curating those people so that we are surrounded by thoughts, words and actions that will nourish us and help us to grow in the way we desire is fundamental to who and how we become.

Key Learning Points

You Are the Product of Your Surroundings: The people you spend the most time with shape your thoughts, beliefs, and behaviours, so it's vital to choose them wisely.

Negativity is Contagious: Negative influences, whether from colleagues, media consumption, or personal relationships, can drain your mental energy and harm your wellbeing.

Curate Your Environment: Conduct a 'people audit' to identify relationships that contribute positively or negatively to your life. Address harmful relationships with compassion and honesty, but accept that you cannot force others to change. Reduce exposure to negative media, such as news and dramatic TV shows, and replace them with uplifting and inspiring content.

Recognise Everyone is Imperfect: Learn from the positive aspects of role models, but don't place them on a pedestal. Embrace their and your own humanity and imperfections as learning opportunities.

If you want to learn more take a look at:

Shawn Achor's *The Happiness Advantage.* (Book)

Maya Angelou's interviews on resilience and personal growth (available on YouTube).

Bernard M. Bass and Ronald E. Riggio's *Transformational Leadership.* (Book)

Brené Brown's *Daring Greatly.* (Book).

Daniel Goleman's *Emotional Intelligence.* (Book)

Simon Sinek's TED Talk: *Start With Why,* on the influence of environment and relationships in driving purpose.

Chapter Five

Listen to Those 'Difficult' Voices

The one where I reflect on the importance of listening to and learning from different, challenging, or contrary voices, and how embracing them can lead to better decisions, personal growth, and stronger leadership.

I have made lots of mistakes in my life, and I'm not ashamed to say it. I have even made the same mistake more than once before I learned from it, and while this chapter could be all about the value of allowing yourself to make mistakes, it's not. It is about some very valuable learning that I got from a repeated mistake.

I seem to be reminded on a regular basis of something I consider to be one of my biggest work-based mistakes. This isn't because it resulted in a disaster that everyone knew about and tried to resolve – far from it – but because I see and hear people repeating the mistake all the time. And I can't guarantee I won't ever make this mistake again. In some ways, what I did was probably human nature; however, I'm definitely much more aware of it now and I try to make sure that I don't fall into that trap again.

The first time I made this mistake, I was a very new manager. In fact, I was still on the NHS Graduate Management Training Scheme. I had been tasked with something that, unbeknown to my bosses, was a dream job for me. We were opening a new wing of a hospital and it had a space for a café. I first got to see the space in early January 2001. It was an empty shell with a tap on the wall, and I was told that my bosses wanted it transformed into a fully functioning café by the time the new wing opened in March. Well, if there's two things this woman loves, it's a challenge and a deadline, so I sprang into action.

The decision had been taken before I started my role that the trust wanted an independent café, not a franchise of one of the large coffee chains, so we were able to create the ambiance, menu, and pricing to suit our needs. It was a busy, but glorious, few months and I learned a lot.

I had a small team consisting of two junior management trainees and had access to the existing catering department staff. One member of the catering team was generally considered to be a very unpleasant individual. They had a reputation as a bully and as a misogynist. I was advised by more experienced managers to keep them away from the project as they didn't have the right vision for it and would drag the whole thing down. So, being new and impressionable, and not particularly liking this individual when I interacted with them, that's exactly what I did. I excluded them and spoke to others to get specialist advice and support. When the individual did try to make an input, I found their views to be way off the mark. They just didn't get what we were trying to create so I ignored them.

Within days of opening, however, we discovered a few operational issues. The proximity of the dishwasher to the till created problems when the café was busy, and the smoke from the panini toaster created ventilation issues. Nothing was unsurmountable, but this could all have been avoided if I'd had an experienced caterer involved in the design. The excluded individual had a vast amount of knowledge but we didn't benefit from it because I chose not to involve them in the work.

Perhaps, if I'd taken the time to work out what was behind their behaviour, I could have improved the situation for all involved, although I acknowledge that this may well have been beyond my ability. Even if that wasn't possible, though, I'm sure we would have been more successful if I'd found a way to tap their knowledge and handle their negativity and behaviour, rather than learning things the hard, and more expensive, way. There is also the chance that, had I interacted with this individual more and they exhibited certain behaviours on me, or in my presence, the organisation would have been able to deal with them appropriately. So, many opportunities were missed thanks to my decision to exclude and ignore them.

The second occasion was with a very different individual, when I worked for a different organisation. Again, they were a manager but this time they were quite mild, kind, and not really a threat to anyone, but they were incredibly boring and usually negative: the type of person that takes fifteen minutes to describe making a ham sandwich, and by the time they have finished you want to smash the sandwich to smithereens! People in the room would start to fidget within thirty seconds of them beginning to talk, and stopped listening soon afterwards. Any input they gave was lost and the general energy level would drop for the rest of the meeting.

Part of my role was to lead a project where I had minimal subject knowledge. I gathered a team of people who understood elements of the processes we were looking to improve. The logical thing would have been to include this individual and draw on their vast knowledge in their particular area. But I just couldn't face it. My colleagues couldn't face it. Rather than speaking with the person and explaining how their tendency to give too much detail, their inability to be brief, and their insistence on focusing only on the risks and drawbacks impacted on the rest of us, I marginalised them. I marginalised this individual with incredible knowledge and commitment simply because I didn't have the bravery, time, or energy to engage with them. This time the project was successful and the ways in which their knowledge could have helped were less stark; however, the process could have been much smoother and less complicated if I'd found a way to harness their knowledge, something I hope I'd find the courage and skill to do now. I also know that the person was aware that they had been excluded from the work. Age and experience have allowed me to think about the impact this could have had on them. This was, remember, a well-meaning, committed colleague who just wanted the best for the organisation and for patients. Keeping them on the outskirts of the project will have had an impact on them – perhaps on their confidence and their sense of self, probably on their professional pride, possibly on their happiness, and I regret that deeply. They did not deserve that treatment.

So, these are two examples of when it seemed easier to avoid the difficult voice rather than to embrace it and hear what it has to teach me. Now I'd like to give some more recent examples of when I've leaned into the experience and opened myself up to contrary views.

I was at an event that included a panel discussion. There were three panellists. Two were completely unknown to me but there was one individual on the panel that I'd had passing contact with and knew of their politics and reputation through social media. None of this particularly aligned with me, my way of doing things, or my values. In fact, when I saw ahead of the event that this person was on the panel I actually rolled my eyes and sighed.

When the panel started, each panellist was asked a question that allowed them to introduce themselves. Two of them gave an adequate and non-irritating (to me) response, including the person I'd been anticipating I would find difficult to listen to. The third panellist spoke about their work and used analogies that suggested that their values and behaviours were starkly different to mine. I felt the muscles in my back tense, one of my signals of discomfort, and had to tell myself to reserve judgement and force myself to really listen to what they were saying. As the panel progressed, this individual continued to show that they were very different to me in their approach, beliefs, and attitudes. But rather than dismissing them outright, I kept listening, for a couple of reasons:

Confirmation bias: One of the lessons I've learned in the past decade has been the danger of confirmation bias. At various times, people have surrounded themselves with people who thought like them, and have only ever heard things that confirmed their beliefs and value system. A good example of this was the Brexit referendum in the UK. Many Remain voters were shocked by the result, as they believed that most people recognised the value of being part of the European Union. Many Leave voters expressed reasons for leaving that actually had nothing to do with the EU and that were based on disinformation – but everyone around them 'knew' and believed in these reasons. So, when I listened to this very different voice, to someone who appeared very different to me, I was ensuring that I wasn't operating in a bubble where everyone was aligned with me.

Learning: There is learning in most exchanges and experiences, and this can sometimes be even more true when those exchanges and experiences are prickly ones. By this I mean that, if we interact with someone who is fully or mainly aligned to us, we can slip into a level of comfort that means that we're not as alert to learning as we could be. When the conversation is prickly, a little difficult to navigate without our views and feelings getting poked, we are more vigilant, so perceiving learning points becomes easier, as long as we keep ourselves open to them. We have to make sure that we listen to hear and not to respond. Listening to respond is a common reaction in most people as we craft our reply while the person is still speaking. However, it's important that we master the skill of listening to hear, as that will allow us to see and understand different perspectives before we accept or reject them.

So I stayed in 'listen' mode, and I'm glad I did. I learned a few things:

We had something in common: Our belief that personal time was important and that we had to switch off from work to be our best. The way that we described that and what we chose to do with our personal time, and why, was very different, but I had to admire the way this very driven individual was clear that #hustle247 was not a way to build an enduring business – and life.

The mode of leadership: A way of doing business that I believed was outdated was still very much alive and well, and that people were happy to pay to learn how to be better at doing things that way. On reflection, this was, of course, obvious; however, it was good to have this reminder of the fact. It helps to put people's experiences into context and to inform the way in which I interact with the business world in the various roles I hold.

My values and beliefs: These, and the behaviours that are rooted in them, are right for me. At no point did the panellist's views make me doubt or question these. Yet the extent to which their expressed beliefs and experiences differed from mine meant that I had to open my mind to diverse viewpoints. Their words, which were backed by their actions later in the event, gave me confidence that the way I choose to lead and the way I choose to do business is the right way for me.

Now I want to move on to the other panellist. Remember them? They were the one I rolled my eyes over when I found out they were on the panel. Listening to them was the greatest revelation of all. This individual, who thinks differently to me politically, and probably ideologically, who I believed was a certain type of leader, about whom I'd only heard things that confirmed my views (remember confirmation bias?), showed themselves to be someone I would be happy to have a proper conversation with – and learn from. They showed that they had reflected on their leadership style, and continue to learn and grow. They openly shared an experience that didn't, at face value, show them at their best, but it highlighted their openness to show vulnerability and to take direct and critical feedback. They demonstrated a maturity of approach and behaviour that I hadn't seen before.

I could have written off this panellist straight away. Had they been the sole speaker, I would have been tempted not to book a place. But being prepared to listen to and include some difficult voices allowed me to see them in a new light, and to learn from them.

Today, in my CEO role, I regularly try to invite in the contrary views and the difficult voices. To end this section, I'd like to share some of my reflections on that experience.

It's difficult

Hearing from people who disagree with you or hold a very different perspective from you can raise all kinds of 'antibodies' in your system. I often have a physiological response to disagreement, especially when it's over something I care deeply about. It's hard not to take disagreement personally and to keep an open mind. Our instinct is to feel like we're being attacked, and to go into the 'freeze, fight, flight, or fawn' response.

If 'flight' wins out, then you will most likely just back down. This might be just the right response. I've been in situations where I've had a thought or an idea that I've been very keen on, then one of the people in the team with more expertise tells me why my idea isn't great. Despite my disappointment, the correct thing for me to do is admit that I was wrong and concede.

Then there's the 'fight' response. Responding aggressively to challenging opinions is unsurprisingly not the most productive strategy. Engaging in a thorough and respectful debate about a topic, and taking time to consider various perspectives, can help you work out if opposing viewpoints are valid or simply expressions of personal biases. The aggressive aspect of the 'fight' response can be a particular problem for leaders, as it may be perceived as an abuse of authority and power. It is important for leaders to manage their 'fight' response by taking a moment to breathe and consider their words before responding. Framing responses as questions to encourage further discussion and acknowledging contributors for their input and challenges can help to develop a more constructive dialogue.

The 'freeze' response is probably the least common, and can be embarrassing. It is often triggered by an unexpected challenge. I can remember times when everyone I've spoken to has thought that something was a good idea that would only improve things for everyone, and then someone has come in with their difficult voice and blindsided me. In these circumstances I can only advise a couple of things. The first is try to avoid this in the first place by checking who you have spoken to: is it a diverse enough group of voices and perspectives? The next is to try to buy yourself some time by taking those views away to consider them. Thank the contributor and tell them you'll need to think about what they've said.

The 'fawn' response may be a new one to you. I've only recently heard of it myself, although I recognise that I have actually done it in the past. The 'fawn' response leads us to be submissive and obedient in the face of danger or challenge. We will go out of our way to appease and please the 'aggressor' rather than prioritising our own wellbeing. This response is often seen in abusive situations, in which the person being abused tries to pacify and placate their abuser. In a work setting, it's most likely to be triggered when someone comes into contact with someone who is very confident (particularly if they themselves have little self-confidence), or someone is demanding, or a bully. The most important step here is to recognise that this is what you are experiencing. Try to form some boundaries, such as saying no, and build a support network that can help you deal with this. If it's triggered by inappropriate behaviours, then, of course, I'd advise you to report it, but I acknowledge that this can be easier said than done – having a support network helps. You might also want to consider, if you experience this response a lot, whether you have other traumas that this response could be linked to. If so, do seek some help for them.

Remember your role

As I mentioned above, your role and seniority in any situation has a huge impact on how easy it is to get those difficult voices to speak, and on how your response is perceived. If you are in a position of power, this affects every interaction with people you have 'power over'. It took me some time to recognise this, as I've never thought of myself as being a 'power over' type of leader; however, the reality is that as a CEO or as a first-level manager, I had power over the people who reported to me. The extent of that power is obviously significantly greater in my CEO role. Even though I am not a hierarchical leader, others' perception of me and my authority will impact on their behaviour around, and towards, me. So you might have to work extra hard to make sure you find those difficult voices (although I've often found them easily enough), and you will certainly have to work on self-management when difficult views are being expressed, to ensure that you balance openness and a willingness to hear and adapt with a perception of weakness and indecision. We also need to be aware that upward bullying exists. Being receptive to difficult voices is not giving staff permission to harass and bully you.

Just because you're open to hearing the voices doesn't mean you have to agree with them

As I've described, listening to different voices and views is a great thing for many reasons. You might hear new solutions to a problem, it can challenge your perceptions and prejudices, and you can learn a great deal. However, the point of listening is not necessarily to get a consensus or compromise. It's not about you giving way to the contrary view. Listening to and really hearing the views that are being expressed may result in you making some changes, but that's not mandatory. It's OK to hear and to consider and then to disregard the viewpoints if it's justified. You are allowed to make decisions, and the fact that some people will disagree with them doesn't mean it's the wrong decision. You will need to consider how you do this and what feedback you give, though, to ensure that this doesn't result in a 'well, next time I won't bother because they don't listen anyway' response.

The voices aren't actually difficult; they're just different

I know that I've used the phrase 'difficult voices' throughout this chapter, because that's how we often see them. In most of the cases I describe above, the individual has also presented with some challenging behaviours, values, and traits. But it's important to reframe 'the difficult voice' to 'a different voice'. What makes a voice 'difficult' is its impact on us and on what we want to achieve. It's about the way in which we receive the voice and our perceptions. It's quite possible that the person owning the 'difficult voice' also finds our voice and views just as difficult to receive! If we think about these voices as 'different' or 'diverse' rather than as 'difficult', we are lifting some of the stigma we've placed on them. It makes us more open to hearing what they are saying, and it encourages us to invite more different and diverse voices in.

Key Learning Points

Different, Not Difficult: Reframe the concept of 'difficult voices' as 'different voices' to encourage openness and reduce stigma, making it easier to invite diverse perspectives into conversations.

The Value of Contrary Opinions: Listening to voices that challenge your views can provide new insights, solutions, and learning opportunities.

Avoiding Confirmation Bias: Surrounding yourself with like-minded people can create an echo chamber that limits growth. Actively seek out opposing viewpoints to broaden your understanding.

The Role of Leadership in Inclusion: Leaders have a responsibility to ensure that all voices, especially those that are quieter or contrary, are heard and valued. Power dynamics impact how difficult voices are expressed and perceived, and leaders must actively work to manage these dynamics constructively.

Listen to Hear, Not to Respond: True listening requires pausing your internal dialogue and focusing on understanding the speaker's perspective rather than preparing your rebuttal.

It's OK to Disagree: Listening doesn't mean you must agree or compromise. It's about considering diverse perspectives before making informed decisions.

If you want to learn more take a look at:

The Arbinger Institute's *Leadership and Self-Deception*. (Book)

Bernard M. Bass and Ronald E. Riggio's *Transformational Leadership*. (Book)

Brené Brown's talks on vulnerability and courage in leadership. (available on YouTube)

Forbes' *How To Use The Power Of Active Listening To Boost Your Career Now*. (Article)

Daniel Goleman's *Emotional Intelligence*. (Book)

Harvard Business Review's *How to Navigate Difficult Conversations with Employees*. (Article)

Patrick Lencioni's *The Five Dysfunctions of a Team*. (Book)

Kim Scott's *Radical Candor*. (Book)

Simon Sinek's TED Talk: *Why Good Leaders Make You Feel Safe*.

Chapter Six

When One Door Closes...

The one where I reflect on embracing setbacks and closed doors throughout my career and how this can lead to unexpected opportunities, personal growth, and a redefinition of success.

What did you want to be when you grew up?

Where did you imagine you'd be now?

What do you aspire to achieve?

I like to look at my career as a series of closing and opening doors. Doors close on one episode or opportunity, and they can open to another stage or role.

I've already spoken about my childhood dreams to become an actor/singer/dancer, and how I pretty much gave up that dream and closed the door on it aged twenty. I then had a four-year gap during which I worked in various customer service roles, in a building society, in a call centre, for an office furniture company, and in short-term (temp) administrative roles. I was almost twenty-four when I first got a taste of working for the NHS.

My introduction to the NHS was serendipitous. I was unemployed and doing short-term roles through an agency when I discovered that Freeman Hospital Liver Unit in Newcastle upon Tyne needed a clerk typist to cover a vacancy for three months. My Mam was a medical secretary and mentioned that I was looking for work. After the shortest of interviews, and based on Mam being excellent at her role, a door opened and I was given the job (this was before robust recruitment processes were really a thing).

Within a couple of weeks, I was hooked. This work mattered. It really mattered. The unit dealt with life and death and made a real difference to the lives of the people it supported. Had this been a fairy tale, I might have applied for the permanent role, got the job, and worked there as a valued member of the team. But I actually realised I loved the work about a week after the closing date for the vacancy, so that door was closed. However, I did apply for, and got, a job as a relief medical typist, which involved covering for medical secretaries' annual leave and sickness. One of these posts was covering the long-term sick leave for the secretary to one of the consultant cardiothoracic surgeons, a post I was then successful in securing when the previous medical secretary didn't return from their sick leave, leaving an open door for me.

Much later, once I had completed the NHS Graduate Management Training Scheme, I was seconded into a role as directorate manager for theatres, the intensive care unit (ICU) and waiting lists. I held that role for two years, during which time I managed to get the budget under control, address a couple of significant waiting-time issues, and improve safety. Most importantly, the team, which had been a disparate, combative group, developed into a supportive team that worked together. When the role was advertised as a permanent post I applied for it, was interviewed, but didn't get the job. My feedback was that I was definitely appointable, but that there had just been someone better on the day.

I was gutted. The team was gutted. So, imagine my surprise when I returned from holiday a few weeks later to be told by the team that the person who'd been appointed had withdrawn from the role. They were convinced that I would now be offered the role. A full week later, a member of the HR team told me that the role was vacant again, that they would be readvertising it and that I was welcome to apply. Welcome to apply?! No, thank you. They obviously didn't want me for the job, and my dream of being a senior operational hospital manager ended. Door closed.

At this point, I almost left the NHS. I was hurt and shocked. I felt unvalued and unwanted. However, something someone said to me convinced me to stay. They told me that something better was in line for me – I just had to give it time. A few months later, when the role of Assistant Director of Operations at North East Ambulance Service was advertised, I applied and got the job. This role gave me the opportunity to be innovative and to work across the entire north-east health and care system. I was freed from a narrow internal perspective, able to spread my wings in a much bigger arena. I learned a lot, made some great contacts, and discovered a world beyond the hospital doors. A new door was open.

Jump forward a few years again. This time I was seconded into the role of assistant director with the organisation that planned and paid for health services (a primary care trust). The role was to develop a clinical commissioning group which was the organisation that was to replace the one I was working in, and to work on urgent and emergency care across the north-east of England. The organisation I was seconded to was coming to an end (door shuts) and the ambulance service had restructured my role out of existence (door slams). So I applied for the role of director of transformation for Northumberland Clinical Commissioning Group.

To me, this seemed like the next logical step. I'd been an assistant director for several years by this time and was strategic and transformational in my thinking and behaviour, and this role would allow me to influence and develop services to meet patients' needs and improve the system. But I didn't get the job; it was given to someone with 'more experience' than me. Another door shut.

They did, however, want me to be their head of governance (a role I'd been fulfilling as part of my development work with them). I couldn't think of anything worse. I understand the importance of good governance and greatly admire those who make it their careers, but it wasn't for me. So they developed a role that combined governance with engagement, organisational development, and planning, which appealed far more, and that was the next door that opened for me.

Two years later, for various reasons, I wanted, or maybe needed, to leave my role, but every time I applied for a different NHS job it was made clear to me that I was going to struggle to progress within the NHS. I didn't fit. It felt like an incredibly heavy, castle-like door was being shut in my face. The only option I could see was to leave the

NHS completely, so I prepared to set up my own business. And then a wonderful door opened into the voluntary and community sector (VCSE) and I stepped through it to become the CEO of Healthwatch Newcastle, which I did alongside my coaching and consultancy business. I continued in this role for over five years before taking up my current position as CEO at St Oswald's Hospice and learned so much about the VCSE as well as continuing to refine and develop my skills and reputation as a leader.

So, why have I shared all of this with you?

When I gave up my dream of being a performer I felt as if my world had ended. But I now teach dance and perform, albeit at a much older age than I would have done had I pursued that career in my early twenties. I also may never have found the passion that I have for public service. I wouldn't have met some of the incredible people I have in my life, and I wouldn't have experienced any of the moments that have made an impact on me and others.

If I'd secured the role as a directorate manager I wouldn't have moved into the ambulance service and interacted with the world outside the acute sector and the NHS. I wouldn't have understood so well how interconnected the system of health, social care, and welfare needed to be in order to get better outcomes for people's health and wellbeing. And I wouldn't be trained to drive an ambulance on blue lights (one of my least useful but most exciting qualifications).

If I'd been successful in my application to become director of transformation, there is a strong possibility that I'd still be enmeshed in the NHS. I'm fairly certain that, had that been the case, I wouldn't have learned to manage imposter phenomenon, I wouldn't feel as safe to advocate for those who need support and are minoritised, I wouldn't have the emotional resilience I now have, and I wouldn't have learned that busy-ness is not a thing to be proud of.

No Pollyannas here

Leaders so often feel that they have to present a brave face all the time. It's tempting to always try to take away the positives in a Pollyanna fashion: to always be optimistic and look for the good in everything. That is not what I am advocating. When our plans don't work out, it's important that we acknowledge the disappointment and the associated pain. There is no shame in being vulnerable.

This canter through some lowlights of my career might make it seem as though I quickly moved on to the next thing, always trying to draw some success from the jaws of failure. However, in reality, the process of learning that not succeeding and not always getting what I wanted wasn't the disaster that I'd imagined took a long time, even if finding the new job only took a few months. The gap between not getting the directorate manager role and being appointed as assistant director with the ambulance service was a little over three months. However, it was probably a couple of years before I recognised just how fortunate I was not to have been appointed to the hospital job. During those months and years I mourned what I had lost while enjoying the challenge of the new position.

I had an unspoken ambition to be a hospital CEO. It was something that was nourished during my time on the NHS Graduate Management Training Scheme and that, while I didn't have a clear career plan, I was mentally working towards. Accepting that this ambition was never going to be achieved took years. I railed against it, trying to make it not so. I threw myself into applications for wholly unsuitable roles in unsustainable places, desperate to get a foot back on the ladder to hospital leadership. It may have been one of the factors that made me keen to be a hospital non-executive director: a chance to operate at that level and reconnect with my hospital roots, even though I was no longer yearning for that top job.

Each time I failed to get my foot back on that hospital CEO ladder, the process was emotionally taxing. I had been rejected or I had discarded my idea of who I wanted to be. That's never an easy thing to deal with. I did look for positives in each situation to ease me through the most painful moments and, a bit like when you go through a relationship break-up, I focused on everything I would have disliked or that would have been difficult if I had got the job. But the disappointment and, at times, the shame was still there, underlying it all and that's what I would return to.

It's important that we know that when we really want something, or really love something or someone, and that thing ends, it is OK to feel loss and to experience sorrow. That's normal. It's OK to feel angry; that's normal. It's OK to feel relieved; that's normal. It's OK to feel lost; that's normal. It's OK to feel all or none of these emotions, or completely different ones, individually or at the same time; that's normal. It doesn't mean you're doing it wrong.

The door will open

I recently held another position, independently of my role as CEO at St Oswald's Hospice, but experiences there, which I'll go into in more detail in Chapter 7, have felt like another door has been slammed in my face. That door was the strongest and heaviest by far. I pictured it like one of those bank safe doors you see in films: over a foot thick with huge bolts and a large turning lock. It shook me to the core as it slammed, and I struggled to stay on my feet for a while.

When this door slammed in my face, however, things were a little different. I had learned that that as one door closes, another opens. While I was in the moment, experiencing all the pain, doubt, anger, and, yes, embarrassment, when I was at my most shaky and unsteady, I told myself that another door would open soon. That knowledge brought me some comfort, in the same way that a painkiller can give temporary pain relief. It made things more manageable and helped me to think and strategise more clearly.

This closed door has given me an opportunity to reflect on the journey I have been on over the past three years, how I got onto that path, and what I can learn from it. This has given me some insights into power inequality, diversity, vulnerability, and allyship, and I've shared this in chapter 7. These insights will help me to support others, as well as ensuring that I choose the right door to walk through next time and that the space behind the door is ready and able to receive all that I have to bring.

So, when I share the advice that 'as one door closes, another one opens', I don't do it to belittle your experiences or emotions. I do it so that you can hold the knowledge close when you need it to help you through the tough times.

How to find the open door

Don't rush!

My way of coping with setbacks is to find a solution and move on. The Kübler-Ross[1] grief cycle applies to all types of loss, not just bereavement, as well as reactions to change. My preferred approach is to whizz through the denial stage (what's the point in denying the inevitable?), indulge briefly in anger, spend a little time bargaining (especially when I'm trying to find meaning and reaching out to others), skip through depression (again for me, what's the point in moping about?), and get on to acceptance, explore my options and move on. However, I know that in reality that's not always possible. When, in the past, I told myself that's what I was doing, I was actually just rushing at a solution, any solution, that would make me feel better. Unfortunately, that solution often just led to another problem and some unresolved grief I had to deal with later.

So, take your time. Allow yourself the feelings and don't worry if you go through some of the stages more than once, and not necessarily in that order (it's normal). But keep your eyes open for opportunities that may be hovering nearby.

Find another way

I didn't get a degree in the same way that a lot of people do (remember, I dropped out of university after two years). However, I realised once I'd started working for the NHS, and particularly once

1. *The Kübler-Ross Grief Cycle outlines five stages of emotional response to loss: Denial, Anger, Bargaining, Depression, and Acceptance. The model is often used to help understand the emotional process involved in grieving.*

I'd discovered the NHS Graduate Management Training Scheme, that I needed a degree to progress. So, I had to find another way to get a degree. Since I like bite-sized goals to work towards, I chose to do a National Vocational Qualification (NVQ), upgrade that to a Certificate in Education, then upgrade that to an honours degree. It took four years, studying alongside working in a full-time job, and it was tough, but I did it.

If you really want something, then looking for an alternative way to get it is usually a good call. It may take longer and be a lot more difficult, but there's usually more than one way to achieve it.

Relax your parameters

We can be very fixed in our beliefs about what we want. I wanted to be a hospital chief executive, and all my efforts and career planning (to the extent that I planned my career) focused on achieving that. However, over time I started to wonder what it was about the role that attracted me: what did I think I would be able to do as a CEO that I couldn't in other roles? The ability to influence the culture of an organisation was a huge attraction, as was the ability to make a positive impact on the lives of the people who worked for it and used its services. The ability to work across organisational boundaries and influence beyond the confines of my organisation was also something I was keen to be able to do. I also craved a degree of autonomy: to be able to set the organisational strategy.

Once I'd accepted that it probably wasn't going to happen for me, I started to wonder if the role would give me what I wanted (particularly the autonomy), and if it was the only way for me to get those things. The answer to both questions was no.

I also wondered if the goal of being a hospital chief executive was actually what I had really wanted in the first place. While the NHS Graduate Management Training Scheme was excellent, it also came with an unwritten tagline: 'Chief executive in ten years'. So, had I wanted to be a NHS CEO or was my people-pleasing self just taking on another external expectation? Quite possibly.

I have spoken with others who didn't branch out and gain the breadth of experience that I did. They've spoken about getting into a position where moving was too much of a risk, financially and professionally. In essence, they had golden handcuffs keeping them in a certain type of role, or even organisation.

Relaxing my parameters and looking for the things I wanted, rather than a specific role, opened up a whole world of opportunities and has ultimately resulted in me securing a role more suited to my wants and needs. It has allowed me to grow into being the type of leader that I truly want to be.

Trust

It will happen. The door will open.

Key Learning Points:

Opportunities Are Cyclical: Career progression and life aspirations often involve doors closing and new ones opening. Setbacks can lead to unexpected and transformative opportunities.

Embrace the Grief of Loss: Acknowledge the disappointment, anger, or sadness that comes with missed opportunities or rejected aspirations. These emotions are a natural part of moving forward.

Look Beyond Rejection: Reframing setbacks as redirections can uncover new paths that align more closely with your values, strengths, and aspirations.

Adaptability Is Key: When a desired path is blocked, finding alternative routes can lead to fulfilling outcomes.

Relax Your Parameters: Focusing on what you truly want from a role, rather than being tied to a specific title or position, can reveal broader opportunities and greater satisfaction.

Trust the Process: Even when faced with the heaviest of closed doors, trust that another door will open and that the journey will lead to growth and alignment with your purpose.

If you want to learn more take a look at:

Bernard M. Bass and Ronald E. Riggio's *Transformational Leadership*. (Book)

William Bridges' *Transitions: Making Sense of Life's Changes*. (Book)

Brené Brown's TED Talk: *The Power of Vulnerability*.

Daniel Goleman's *Emotional Intelligence*. (Book)

Sheryl Sandberg and Adam Grant's: *Option B: Facing Adversity, Building Resilience, and Finding Joy*. (Book)

Simon Sinek's TED Talk: *Start With Why*

Chapter Seven

Not Every Table Feeds You

The one where I show that not every table is worth sitting at and the importance of choosing inclusive spaces that truly value diversity and foster meaningful contributions.

A few years ago, I was invited to apply for a Board-level position in a prestigious organisation. But first let me go back a few steps. I was contacted by someone I'd interacted with quite a lot on social media, who worked for this organisation, asking if I'd be available for a chat. I agreed and we had a great telephone conversation in which he explained to me that the chair of the organisation had approached him, an ethnically minoritised man, to ask if he was aware of any ethnically diverse people who might be suitable to apply for a Board post. He wanted to check that I was OK with him putting my name forward. I was extremely flattered and told him that I would definitely be OK with that. A little while later, my coach, a Black woman, told me that the chair had also approached her to ask if she could suggest anyone; she had also recommended me. How lovely that two people had the same thought about me.

Many months later, I was contacted by the chair themselves. They told me that the Board was looking to have more diverse membership and they wanted to actively recruit a new non-executive director who would bring difference to the Board. They recognised that previous recruitment to these posts had used Board experience as a criterion, and that could be a barrier to attracting applicants from different backgrounds, so they would be looking at things differently this time. We discussed the role and I was excited, and flattered, at the opportunity.

When the role was advertised, I applied, went through a thorough and rigorous recruitment process, and was appointed. To say I was over the moon is an understatement. The organisation had a special place in my heart and has a significant impact across the region, nationally and internationally, so it was a massive opportunity for me to be able to make significant change and impact, and to be able to influence the strategy that could change so many people's experiences.

On my first proper day on the job, at my first Board meeting, I believed I contributed well to the first part of the meeting, bringing insights that my range of work experience had allowed me to gain. Everything seemed to be going well. Then we came to the second part of the Board meeting. We were observed by a number of people, including members of the press. The Board chair welcomed everyone to the meeting then introduced me, saying something like: 'As you may notice, we have a new person around the table, Steph Edusei, who is joining us as a non-executive director. As you can see, she is a person of colour... Pink!', and they laughed.

I wanted the ground to open up and swallow me whole. This was an observed Board meeting, the press was there – what should I do? Should I challenge them on the inappropriateness of their comment? Their chuckle obviously showed me that they thought it was a good joke (my top and my coat on the back of my chair were both pink), but I felt singled out – and not in a good way. I felt like they'd both highlighted and negated my ethnicity. I felt othered. Marginalised. And I did what so many people do in a similar situation, where they are in the minority and an authority figure of the majority says or does something that 'others' them under the guise of a joke. I gave an embarrassed laugh.

For the next five minutes or so (it felt like longer), my mind continued in a whirlwind of:

- 'What should I do?'
- 'What should I say?'
- 'This is not on.'
- 'I'm an advocate for equity and inclusion, and I'm accepting this?'
- 'People are watching.'
- 'I'm so embarrassed.'

Eventually, I gave myself a talking-to and told myself to focus or I'd add no value to the meeting. I resolved to mention it to the chair at another time, but events overtook me and I bumped into them shortly after at a large social event. As we passed, they raised what they'd said and that they'd thought it was a rather good joke. Again I gave an embarrassed laugh, then they moved on. I'm ashamed that I never challenged them on it.

For the next few years, I felt placated, gaslighted, and ignored. When I raised concerns about racism and misogyny brought to me by staff I was told I was misinformed, that the claims were exaggerated, that they had been dealt with (they hadn't), or that they were rooted in poor performance. I was told that the organisation was working very hard to address these issues, and yet worsening statistics and experiences suggested these efforts weren't working. I don't believe I saw any recognition of this. I had a couple of allies around the table who would step up and speak, but if they weren't there I felt alone. I felt that any attempts I made to encourage dialogue and learning were met with deaf ears or what seemed to me like obfuscation.

I have many examples of the challenges this caused. At times, I was in tears, despairing that staff trusted me and confided in me about the challenges and discrimination they were facing, yet I was struggling to have my voice heard and to make a difference. I had conversations with my partner about the fact I might have to step away at some point, because I didn't want to be associated with an organisation that didn't take action – but then if I wasn't there saying this stuff, who would? In the end, events overtook me and most of the non-executive directors, myself included, were asked to step down from the Board. That in itself was a painful process for me, as I felt I was letting people down and that I'd lost the valuable and important seat at the table that would have allowed me to make positive change. However, with time, reflection and some healing, I've realised something important – I was never welcome at the table.

If I look back to my initial conversation with the chair, remove the rosy glow that flattery and excitement added, and recall the actual words used, they went along the lines of: '[Overarching organisation] is going to make Boards become more diverse, so we've decided that we want to get ahead of the game and are looking to recruit a non-executive director from a more diverse background.'

They said nothing about why they wanted to be more diverse, or about what benefits it would bring them and the organisation. It was all about the fact that they were probably going to have to do it at some point, so they may as well do it now. I truly believe that what many of them thought they were getting in me was a compliant light-skinned Black woman with a soft Geordie accent; someone who was just like them... but with a bit of a tan.

Once I'd put my experiences in that context and, supplemented by conversations I've had with some amazing people, including on my *Black All Year* podcast[1], I now understand that being asked to have a seat at the table is not the right objective.

What's important is being included at the right table.

Has the table done the work?

I've heard and seen too many examples of people being given a role within an organisation, only to face the same types of prejudice and discrimination I saw and experienced. The people in the organisation think they're open and inclusive, but they haven't taken the time to consider their biases and the behaviour and barriers they lead to. They haven't taken a look at their practices and policies to see if they are welcoming to people from different backgrounds and cultures or with different needs, and then made changes to ensure they're inclusive.

When I worked at the ambulance service, one of the ambulance stations had a women's changing room which was a converted cupboard, because it had never entered anyone's mind that they might have a woman working there. I don't know when the changing room was created, but I'm willing to bet it was after women were recruited and someone had the afterthought that they might need a place to go to the loo and change their clothes. Years later, nothing had changed and the women continued to use the less-than-adequate facilities. Not exactly welcoming.

Policies tend to be designed around a western European approach to families and culture; for example, bereavement policies that only recognise parents, siblings, and children as immediate family, or dress codes that don't allow for protective hairstyles in Black hair such as braids or locks. Or we see half-hearted attempts at inclusion that show that organisations haven't taken the time to truly understand the needs of others, such as guidance on supporting fasting staff through Ramadan but not allowing staff the flexibility to take a day off for Eid.

And then we have the micro-aggressions.

For those that don't know, a micro-aggression is usually described as a comment or action that subtly, and often subconsciously, shows a biased attitude towards someone from a marginalised group. Many people dislike the term 'micro-aggression' because it can imply that the experience is minor, despite its significant and cumulative impact. 'Exclusionary behaviours' is probably a more accurate term to use.

Whatever we choose to call them, these behaviours, like my introduction at the Board meeting, may be subconscious but they are damaging and create an atmosphere of exclusion and discrimination. Organisations, and the people within them, have to take the time to learn about exclusionary behaviours, how they might show up, and how to avoid and tackle them – before someone joins who might be impacted by them. The chair could have introduced me and mentioned the fact that I was from an ethnically minoritised background in an inclusive way. They could have said something like: 'We're delighted to welcome Steph to the Board, because not only does she bring a wealth of experience from across health and the voluntary and community sectors, but she will also be able to bring a range of new perspectives as a Black woman and EDI (equality, diversity and inclusion) advocate that will support better decision-making and help us to better meet our patient and staff needs.' That type of introduction recognises the skills, experience, and benefits I bring rather than making a joke about my ethnicity.

While I am ashamed I didn't challenge the chair about their comment about me at that first Board meeting, I also realise it probably wouldn't have made a great deal of difference and, in fact, could have made my position even more difficult.

Why does the table want you to sit at it?

- A desire to diversify the Board or organisation is not a valid reason for inviting people to the table.
- A need to fill a quota is not a valid reason for inviting people to the table.
- A fear of backlash or a loss of customer base is not a valid reason for inviting people to the table.
- A desire to be more representative of the population you serve is, I'd argue, not a valid reason for inviting people to the table.

It is important that you take time to consider and recognise the value that diversity brings, and how that will benefit your organisation in particular. What will the table get from being more diverse?

Creativity: Diverse teams generally think more creatively and use their differing backgrounds and experiences to find solutions to problems.

Better decision-making: Diverse teams are more likely to make better decisions because they have a variety of perspectives and ideas.

Improved cultural awareness: Diverse teams are better placed to understand the different nuances and influences within a multicultural or global marketplace.

Stronger business results: Diverse teams generally lead to stronger business results and profits.

Improved employee retention: Employees are more likely to remain loyal when they feel respected and valued for their unique contribution.

Better understanding of customers: Diverse teams are able to better understand their customers by drawing on their variety of perspectives and experiences.

Improved reputation: Companies with diverse workplaces are often perceived as better employers.

Continuous learning: Diverse teams can create an environment where employees can learn from one another.

Understanding and appreciating these benefits will help you to create a true desire for diversity that will ensure that you invite people to your table for the right reasons, and make it more likely that they will feel welcome, included, and valued once they arrive.

Before I move on to the next question, I want to explain why a desire to be more representative of the population you serve is not, to my mind, a valid reason to invite people to the table.

Let's imagine you operate in an area where the population is 98% white with no visible LGBTQIA+ community – there are lots of such areas in the UK. If you are representative of your population, then it would be absolutely fine to have all white, straight people on the Board. However, in this situation you'd be missing out on the fact that visibility isn't everything (how can you see someone's sexual orientation, neurodivergence, or, in some cases, their gender?) and the fact that 2% of your population might have a very different perspective and experience than the majority. You'd also be losing the type of benefits from diversity that I mentioned above.

If your aim is to be representative, you will likely do what I describe above. It would make perfect sense to look at the proportions of your population – 24% have a disability, 19.3% are from an ethnically minoritised population, 10.5% are LGBTQIA+, 51% are female – then look to recreate something similar. But that is just a 'painting by numbers' approach that doesn't consider the differences within each of those groups, the intersectionality between them, or the qualities, skills, and experiences that you're really seeking to bring.

A focus on being representative of your population, especially at a Board level, can also put a heavy burden on the people asked to 'represent'. Being representative is, in part, a good thing, but as I often say, I don't represent an entire group of people. I can't possibly do that. How can I possibly represent people I don't know, who I will never meet? Yet that's the position I am put in.

When we're put in that position, we know we are representing everybody in our group and, when that is a minoritised group such as women, ethnically minoritised people, or people with disabilities, in the wrong environment every flaw, every mistake, everything we say can be construed as representing how all people from that minoritised group behave, how 'they' all speak, how 'they' all think. As a result, we have to be mindful of how we portray others from our group on top of all of the other factors we might encounter.

It's also important to remember there are different levels of privilege within and between different minoritised groups. For example,

I know that as a light-skinned Black woman, who is heterosexual, doesn't have a disability, and is educated to a postgraduate level (among many other factors), I hold a lot of privilege. As a result, my experiences will be markedly different from, and better than, that of others who are marginalised and don't hold the same level of privilege. In the same way, my experiences are usually worse and more complex than those of a white woman.

So, really think what you mean by being 'representative', and what is actually driving that, so you can avoid some of the pitfalls I've described.

What is the format/shape of the table?

Here, I mean this literally and figuratively. We send out messages through our choice of furniture without thinking about it.

The traditional meeting table in the Western world is rectangular. Some would say that this is a symbol of authority and strength. In China, a circular table symbolises peace and harmony. At a rectangular table, only the people at the ends have sight of the whole table. On a circular table, pretty much everyone can see each other. Where you sit on a rectangular table and your proximity to others, especially those in authority, makes a difference. Where you sit on a circular table is less significant, but not completely unimportant.

So, the physical shape of a table has significance, and if you want to encourage inclusivity and collaboration then selecting the right table can help.

But furniture isn't magic. Changing from a rectangular table to a circular one won't miraculously transform culture and behaviours.

We also may not have a choice about table shape; money or space may dictate what we can use. So, does that mean that a rectangular meeting table will override actions to create a more equal and inclusive environment? Of course not.

I have a rectangular table in my office, but you'll very rarely see me sitting at the 'head' of that table. To do so would be to send a message to everyone about the type of leadership style I was intending to adopt in that meeting and, while that could very occasionally be an appropriate style, it rarely is for me.

I also try to ensure that people have an equal voice in the teams I lead, so the shape of the table, or even the existence of a table, doesn't matter. Now, this isn't utopia. I'm not naive; I know hierarchy exists and influences how people behave, but I am as keen to hear the views of the lowest paid (but by no means least important) in the organisation as I am those of the Board. In fact, I often find the views and experiences of those who are doing the things we need to do more important than those of the people leading the organisation. Even if their perceptions are shaped by a limited view of the whole picture, that creates their reality, and that's the environment in which I'm expecting them to perform and thrive. It gives vital information that can help us to change their environment or help them to see more of the picture, to put their experience into context and, hopefully, as a result improve their views.

Truly opening yourself up to hearing and involving everyone means you need to have a very large metaphorical table, and you're creating an environment where people know they don't have to wait for an invitation to have a seat. I don't think we're there yet, but that means we just have to keep working at it.

How will the table adapt to make sure everyone has space to sit and stretch their arms?

You know those times when you've been packed around a table like a tin of sardines – think a large meeting in a too-small room, or a meal out with family or friends when the restaurant has given you a table made for four fewer people than you have in your party. No one has space, everyone is invading someone else's space, and you don't feel like you can move or get up without disturbing all the people around you. Well, this is the metaphorical form of that.

- Does everyone around the table have the space, permission, and safety to be themselves?
- Do people welcome different views and perspectives as constructive challenges or innovative thinking, do they tolerate them, or do they shut them down?
- Is the table static? Have the people around it been there for years without changing in any way? Are they stuck in their ways, their views and their outlook?
- Are people allowed to change their perspective and views, or are they ridiculed for being indecisive?
- How do you think the table would react if you wanted to discuss something very different? Would they listen openly, welcome the input, discuss, debate, and consider, or would they shut you down or deny you?

If you just want to sit at the table, take the role and the prestige but make no real difference, then this won't matter to you. You can sit, elbows tucked in, hardly moving unless everyone moves in unison to make sure no one is inadvertently bumped. But if this is what you want, question what value you're bringing to the table and why you should be there rather than a lot of other people just like you. Because I'd argue you will be interchangeable with a huge number of other people who also just want that seat. However, if you've made it to this point in the book, then I suspect that's not what you want at all, so taking time to examine these aspects of the table is time well spent.

How is the table going to create more space for people like you (or those who are different to you but different to everyone else at the table)?

'So we've got a couple of women, a South Asian man and someone who's gay – what a diverse group we are!' Now, not surprisingly no one has ever said that in my presence, but the inference has been there on a few occasions and I know, from speaking with people who say they want to attract diverse people into their organisations or onto their Boards, that this is how too many people think. I've heard people comment on how many people from LGBTQIA+ communities a team may have, how 'women are taking over', or how 'you hardly see any white faces any more'. It's almost as if they have a diversity checklist and mark their teams off against it. Like on a bingo card, when they have checked off all the characteristics they call 'full house'!

If you join a table that has this kind of attitude, then you can be fairly certain that one of the reasons you've been brought in is to fulfil a function or quota, to be the characteristic that was missing. You can also be fairly confident that some of the following things will happen:

- You will be expected to be the fount of all knowledge on anything relating to that characteristic. I've lost count of the number of times I've been asked about how Muslim women may feel about something. Now, I have spent a lot of time engaging with and learning about Muslim practices and cultures, I have friends who are Muslim women, but I am not Muslim or South Asian or Arabic (which is what people actually mean when they say 'Muslim women' – they're not talking about white Geordie women who have converted to Islam). However, as I've already mentioned, some people seem to think that because my skin is brown I must understand the concerns of all of the global majority population.

- Your perspective that comes from your characteristic may be questioned if it's not relating to something that sits within that characteristic's sphere of concern. For example, I'm allowed to comment with authority on things relating to women or ethnically minoritised people, but I would be challenged if I spoke about a business practice, even when that is informed by the cultural and societal experience of being Black and female. In a discussion about developments or plans that have no obvious equality and inclusion aspect to them, I've had significant pushback when I've suggested that different people or groups (e.g. women or people who have experienced racism) might experience things differently. The general feeling has been, they're not talking about 'that stuff', so why have I brought it up. I've also been told that I 'see racism everywhere' (direct quote from someone, although not in a work setting).

- Your contribution to anything else might be questioned or downplayed. I have had roles in the past where it's been made clear that I have a function to perform, and expressing an opinion on other things is outside that function. My authority to speak in that area has been questioned and, in the worst cases, I've been completely ignored.

Is this even a table that you want to be at?

Once you've considered all of the above, how much do you want to be at that table? It may still be the right thing for you to do. It might be an essential element to add to your work experience and help to get you the next role. You may not have a lot of choice – sometimes we're pushed up to the table, whether we want to be there or not. If you think you should be there to make a difference and to make a change, really think about how likely this is. Depending on the above factors, change may not be possible, or the process of stimulating and driving the change could be personally damaging. Be realistic about what is achievable and choose your table carefully, because the right one for you is out there somewhere.

Is this really a rare seat at the table?

I'd like to finish by saying a little something about the concept of scarcity. Many of us are made to believe that the things we want are in short supply – 'good men', great jobs, seats at the table – and as a result we are encouraged to see ourselves in competition with others just like us. As a woman, and especially as a Black woman, this is a message and situation I'm all too familiar with. We see the consequences of this thinking all the time. We see female leaders who are protectionist, who block other potential female leaders, and work against junior women with potential. We see Black people who take on the rhetoric and beliefs of racism and regurgitate it, using it as a weapon against others. We see the undermining and back biting that reflects people desperately trying to attain and hang on to power.

However, the concept of scarcity has been created by the few who already have their seat at the table and want to ensure it stays reflective of them, and that their position and power remain unchallenged.

I'd like to invite you to look at things a little differently. What is in short supply is you. Your talent, skills, experience, and perspective are scarce, they are unique, and they are valuable. What is more, surrounding yourself with, and collaborating with, others only makes you greater and even more valuable. So, if you want to help change the narrative and landscape for minoritised groups, value yourself and choose collaboration over competition.

Don't jump at the first role you are offered because you think opportunities are scarce. There is great strength in being able to turn something down so you can wait for the right opportunity: the one that is right for you and where you thrive.

Key Learning Points

About the Tables You Join: It's not enough to have a seat at the table; the environment, culture, and motives behind inviting you matter just as much.

Why you've Been Invited: Is your inclusion driven by a genuine desire for diverse perspectives and the value they bring, or by tokenism and quotas?

Readiness of the Organisation: Organisations must do the necessary internal work – by addressing biases, exclusionary behaviours, and systemic barriers – before inviting diverse voices to the table.

Representation vs. Inclusion: Representation is not enough if the environment doesn't allow people to thrive, contribute fully, or feel valued for their uniqueness.

Microaggressions/Exclusionary Behaviours: These behaviours, even if they are subtle or unintentional, create environments of exclusion and discrimination.

Scarcity Thinking: Avoid the belief that opportunities are limited. Your unique skills, experience, and perspective are valuable, and the right opportunities will come.

Collaboration Over Competition: Building alliances and supporting others enhances collective progress and resilience rather than competing for scarce opportunities.

Emotional Toll of Being the 'First' or 'Only': Being a representative voice for a minoritised group can come with significant pressures and challenges. Ensure the organisation supports and values your contributions beyond symbolic representation.

If you want to learn more take a look at:

Black All Year. (Podcast)

Jennifer Brown's *How to Be an Inclusive Leader*. (Book)

Catalyst's *The Bottom Line: Connecting Corporate Performance and Gender Diversity*. (Book)

Cultural Intelligence (CQ) Framework: Provides insights into how organisations can adapt to and embrace diverse cultural perspectives.

The Diversity Gap. (Podcast)

Intersectional Leadership: Considers how overlapping identities (e .g., race, gender, class) impact individuals and how leaders can address these intersections to promote equity.

McKinsey & Company's *Diversity Wins: How Diversity, Equity and Inclusion Matter*. (Report)

Servant Leadership: Focuses on prioritising the needs of others, fostering inclusivity, and creating environments where everyone can thrive.

Beverly Daniel Tatum's:*Why Are All the Black Kids Sitting Together in the Cafeteria?* (Book)

Chapter Eight

You Don't Have to Be the Expert

The one where I show that embracing not being the expert leads to fresh perspectives, innovative solutions, and the freedom to learn and contribute in meaningful ways.

In autumn 2024, I was invited to the North East Growth Summit. It was an event hosted by the Northern Powerhouse and the North East Chamber of Commerce and supported by the new mayoral authority of the North East Combined Authority. I knew the room would be full of powerful and influential people; it had been invitation only and was fully booked. However, I was a little taken aback when some of the voluntary and community sector people I had assumed would be there weren't. There were, however, a number of faces I recognised, and I had some nice, casual conversations before the event started.

Within minutes of the first speaker getting up, imposter phenomenon started to rise. What on earth was I doing in that room? It was full of businesspeople, people who worked in the public sector, but not health, and politicians. Health services were not represented, and therefore it was not my usual crowd at all.

I've already talked at length in Chapter 2 about how I allowed imposter phenomenon to influence me for a large part of my life, and, because of all of the work I've done to ensure I don't let it influence my choices, it was quickly surpassed by curiosity about what had triggered it on this occasion. What was it about that space that had led me to the old feelings of not being enough? I knew I had been invited to sit in that room and that what I needed to do was focus on what people were saying, what I could learn, and what my contribution would be, so I let the curiosity linger and allowed myself to accept that I was where I deserved to be.

Not too long afterwards, the new mayor of the north-east, Kim McGuinness, started to speak. She talked about wanting to create an everyday economy, and instantly I knew where my contribution lay. When invited to ask questions, I asked how we could make sure the 'everyday economy' was an 'everyone economy' that left nobody behind and lifted all ships. Kim loved the question, finding it insightful and valid. So, a big part of my role on that day was to make sure that the importance of bringing all sections of our north-east communities on the journey with us was at the forefront of people's minds.

So, why had imposter phenomenon reared its head in that moment? Well, I'd forgotten some of my learning. Imposter phenomenon is more likely to occur when I am in an unfamiliar situation. Nowadays for me that doesn't often mean a new group or a new room, but it does mean a new context, and that is exactly what the summit was. I'm now skilled and confident enough to be able to recognise the voice of self-doubt for what it is, and manage it accordingly. The other bit of learning I had forgotten, and would have helped, is that you don't always have to be the expert in the room.

The power of being a generalist

Throughout most of my career, I have not been an expert. Working in health, there has always been a plethora of healthcare professionals who have studied and practised long and hard to become experts in their field. I would never dream of competing with their knowledge and understanding of their specialist fields. I've always called myself a generalist: I've known a bit about a lot of things, but never specialised in anything.

I have long believed that being a generalist is a real strength. As I see it, the superpower of being a generalist is the freedom to ask 'silly' questions. In my early days of management I would quite frequently say, 'Forgive me, because this is probably a silly question, but...', followed by something that questioned or challenged the status quo. I soon discovered that these questions were powerful because people would be forced to explain things clearly, in layperson's terms, or to recognise that what they were describing was not credible or no longer valid. After all, what is a silly question? Is it a simple enquiry coming from an uncluttered perspective that allows one to cut through rhetoric and assumption? Being a generalist has allowed me to see across and beyond the boundaries of specialisms because I haven't had the in-depth knowledge of particular areas sucking me down into the detail. I haven't known the detail of why things happened in a certain way, the history and the theories that supported it. I've just been able to see that something did, or did not, make sense.

There have been countless occasions when collective wisdom, custom, and practice has meant that things have been done a certain way; a process had to be designed to accommodate individuals, processes, resources, or beliefs. However, when one or more of those factors changed the process remained the same, almost as though a road had been laid around buildings and then those buildings had been demolished but the road endured and people kept following its winding route. For example, a process is designed to ensure that it meets externally set standards. The external standard then changes but the process remains, meaning that people keep doing the same thing for no real purpose. Not being the expert has allowed me to look at the road and wonder why it's like that – and to ask why.

One of my proudest achievements was creating a scheme similar to one the NHS now runs called the Volunteer to Career programme. While working at the ambulance service, we faced a shortage of non-emergency ambulances for transporting patients to appointments and treatments. This led to long journeys for patients and high taxi costs as we had to take circuitous routes and hire private taxis. The commissioners couldn't buy more capacity, leaving us with a low-satisfaction, loss-making service.

When I spoke to the experts in the ambulance service about the challenges of non-emergency transport, they explained to me how routes were put together to maximise capacity, how dropping people off and picking them up in batches helped our efficiency, and while it wasn't ideal for patients, or good for the hospitals, it was the best way to meet the need. They said that, while our taxi use was eye-wateringly high, no taxi was booked that didn't need to be, and we could cancel them if we managed to get patients into one of our own vehicles.

The experts didn't seem to have any solution other than 'buy more vehicles', which would mean more cost.

I spent some time on the road with our non-emergency transport service, and the experts working there told me about the challenges they had with patients not being ready to be collected, and not being where they were supposed to be at the hospital. Those who had worked there for years told me that 'in the old days' hospital porters used to take patients from reception to their appointments, but this was now something the ambulance workers had to do.

Not being an expert in any of this, I was able to ask 'why?'

- Why did we have to do it like this?
- Why had the hospital portering service that could support these patients been removed?
- What did the porters actually do?
- How much time did we lose doing things that weren't strictly ambulance service responsibilities?

We did some research, and discovered that around a third of their time was spent 'portering' patients around the hospital setting.

At the time, there was high unemployment. Those who had been out of work for over a year and were defined as long-term unemployed found it particularly challenging to find new work. I was also a volunteer with Girlguiding UK, and had been for many years. I knew about the benefits of volunteering, and the skills, experience, and confidence it had given me over the years.

Bringing all of this together, I asked another 'silly' question: why can't volunteers meet the patients when they arrive via ambulance and escort them to their appointments, then pick them up after their appointment and take them to the collection point for their ambulance home?

I was told the hospital porters wouldn't stand for volunteers taking their jobs. I asked why they would object if portering these patients wasn't their job. After all they weren't doing it.

I was told volunteers wouldn't want to do that and wouldn't have the training to do that. I asked, 'How do you know?' and 'Why can't we train the volunteers?'

I was told my idea wouldn't free up that much time so it wouldn't be worth the money.

I asked how we could say that when we knew that a third of our drivers' time was spent portering patients: wasn't it worth a try?

We developed a pilot of a volunteer ambulance porter service and worked with a local government employment agency to recruit a number of volunteers who were long-term unemployed. To make sure they were adequately supported, we asked one of our non-emergency transport managers to base themselves in the hospital at which the pilot was to be run from and provide mentorship, training, and support to the volunteers. It worked wonderfully and within weeks:

- We had praise from the hospital, and were asked if we could also train the volunteers in fire evacuation so they could assist, should there be a fire.

- We had positive feedback from patients.
- Our taxi costs plummeted, as efficiency and utilisation of our vehicles rose.
- Our staff were happier, as they were doing what they had joined the service to do, not wandering hospital corridors looking for patients.

There was one 'downside', though. Within months, we had to recruit more volunteers – because two-thirds had secured employment! People who had been unemployed for over a year were able to use the experience, skills, and confidence they acquired through volunteering to help them get permanent employment, mostly within the health and care sector. Perhaps my proudest day was when one of our volunteers got a job with the ambulance service.

Not being an expert and being able to ask these questions helped us to develop a service that, as far as I'm aware, still exists today. The model has been rolled out to many hospitals and, as I mentioned above, is the blueprint for a huge programme supporting volunteering, with a view to bringing people into employment in the NHS. Not being an expert and being able to ask these questions helped people into jobs and helped give purpose to the lives of those who volunteered.

Keeping that inexpert curiosity

Of course, this is a superpower that can diminish. As you become more familiar with a subject area and understand more, it's easy to start accepting the status quo. When I start hearing myself use terms like 'historically' when I'm explaining why something is done a certain way, or stating that something can't be changed without knowing exactly why it can't be changed, I know it's time to reset my non-expert status and to start questioning more.

It's also why I welcome new joiners to our team, telling them that they are even more valuable than usual in this initial phase. They will see things they don't understand or won't see things they'd expect to see, and I encourage them all to ask 'Why?' or 'Why not?' We can see ourselves anew through their 'inexpert' eyes.

The burden of being the expert

Being an expert, or being perceived as an expert, can be really tough.

The definition of an expert is a person who is very knowledgeable about, or skilful in, a particular area. They have mastery of a subject or skill, and they tend to be the people to whom others defer. In many ways, being an expert is a bit like being a CEO – people usually expect you to have all the answers and to get everything right, without understanding the complexity of what you're dealing with and that there often isn't one straightforward 'right' or 'wrong' solution. In health, for example, people often think it's a simple equation:

set of symptoms = condition = known treatment

whereas it's far more complicated than that, and a lot of medicine is about excluding conditions, trying treatments, and seeing how the patient reacts.

So, when you are seen as the expert, you are expected to have the knowledge, skills, and experience that mean you have all the answers. People look to you to explain why and how things have happened, or how they should be. In this context, it can be difficult to say that you're unsure or that you just don't know, especially if you factor in that there is a high likelihood that these experts will also be experiencing imposter phenomenon. Does saying you don't know, that you don't have the answer mean you aren't such an expert after all? Is it a weakness, real or perceived, or a failing? If it is, and if experts are under pressure to be correct and to know the right course of action all the time, what might happen? Experts might give their best (and informed) guess, speaking as if they are certain, and their answer is likely to be taken as fact because it's coming from an expert. They might also double down, become more entrenched in their position, and feel threatened by someone questioning them. Neither scenario is likely to give a great outcome.

Being a non-expert frees you from these expectations and gives you licence to do more than just ask 'silly' questions: it also allows you to be open and to learn.

The North East Growth Summit brought lots of new-to-me concepts and ideas. They were so far outside my realm of knowledge, let alone expertise, that I had a novel experience: I was able to listen, to learn things, without having to filter what speakers were saying through my own experience. It was wonderful to simply listen to hear and learn without any other purpose. It made me recognise one of the benefits of going to events where speakers from lots of different backgrounds share lots of different, unconnected, thoughts, experiences, and expertise. It gives you the gift of not being the expert in the room. It returns you to being a pupil in the classroom, acquiring knowledge and ideas. I found it refreshing and enlightening – and it freed up my own thinking about the issues and challenges I have to deal with.

So, remember that being the expert and gaining experience is amazing. Working to achieve that level of knowledge and skills, then using that in your chosen field is something that is – rightly – applauded and encouraged. We need experts. But when you're an expert in a certain field, you don't have to know everything. Being the generalist in some situations and fields is not a position of weakness: it brings real value and benefit, so don't overlook this. Allow yourself to experience being 'not the expert'. Look for situations where that's the case. Freely acknowledge to yourself, and others, that it isn't your area of expertise, but don't do this from a position of lack. Own the strength this gives you and be confident in your lack of knowledge.

Oh, and a little confession: I used to be a generalist with no particular area of expertise, but that's changed. Remembering that there's always room for improvement, I'm happy to now say I'm expert in leadership.

Key Learning Points

The Power of Generalism: Being a generalist allows you to ask 'silly' questions, cut through assumptions, and explore fresh perspectives that specialists may overlook.

Curiosity Over Expertise: Embracing curiosity can lead to innovative solutions, as it enables questioning the status quo without being anchored by in-depth knowledge of existing processes.

Questioning the Status Quo: Asking 'why' or 'why not' can challenge entrenched practices, unearth inefficiencies, and spark transformative change.

The Value of Inexpert Eyes: Encouraging new team members to question practices with their fresh perspective can help uncover inefficiencies and foster innovation.

The Freedom of Non-Expertise: Not being the expert can liberate you from the burden of always having answers, fostering an environment of openness and collaborative learning.

The Burden of Expertise: Experts often face pressure to know all the answers, which can lead to entrenchment or overconfidence. Acknowledging limits is key to maintaining humility and fostering growth.

Continuous Learning: Seeking out unfamiliar settings and diverse knowledge areas keeps your thinking sharp, refreshes your perspective, and fuels personal and professional growth.

Imposter Phenomenon and Unfamiliar Situations: Feeling like an imposter can resurface in unfamiliar contexts, even for seasoned professionals. Acknowledging this and managing it effectively is a valuable skill.

If you want to learn more take a look at:

Brené Brown's TED Talk: *The Power of Vulnerability*.

David Epstein's *Range: Why Generalists Triumph in a Specialised World*. (Book)

Daniel Kahneman's *Thinking, Fast and Slow*. (Book)

Simon Sinek's *Leaders Eat Last*. (Book)

Chapter Nine

If This Were True...

The one where I explore how embracing even the most challenging feedback with curiosity and humility can lead to growth, learning, and stronger leadership.

In early summer 2023, the Care Quality Commission (CQC) descended onto Newcastle Upon Tyne Hospitals for an inspection and it was tough. The inspection would usually take a few days, or at most a couple of weeks for larger organisations, but it continued for months and involved significant input from the leadership team and staff alike.

For anyone who doesn't know, the CQC is the independent regulator of health and adult social care services in England. All services have to be registered with the CQC, and they undergo periodic inspections of all or part of their services, which results in a rating. The ratings go from 'Inadequate', which usually results in significant national intervention, to 'Outstanding'.

Within a few weeks of the start of the inspection at Newcastle, we had some initial negative feedback. There were mixed reactions to this across the leadership team. Some of the team found it challenging to accept this. I was part of a small group of people who weren't surprised by the feedback, as we had heard from staff and tried to share our concerns about similar matters, but that made it no easier to hear. Some people expressed sorrow and concern; others displayed disbelief and defensiveness.

The latter response made me think about how difficult it can be to hear negative feedback about ourselves or our work, especially if we disagree with that feedback, or perhaps even more so if it hits a sensitive spot. I recognised that when someone gives what we feel to be unfair or incorrect criticism it's easy to dismiss it, condemn the person or organisation sharing the feedback, and move on. I saw this frequently in my days at Healthwatch and in the NHS. Organisation A would give feedback to Organisation B about how the way in which its service was designed negatively impacted Organisation A's ability to deliver its services. Organisation B would respond with counter-criticism and defensiveness. A patient or carer would complain about their experience of using the services, only to be met with passive-aggressive responses like 'I'm sorry you felt the need to complain...', as if their complaint wasn't valid. This was also usually accompanied by internal comments about unrealistic expectations. As I've mentioned elsewhere, feeling as if you are being attacked is quite natural, and our response is on based in the instinctive 'fight, flight, freeze, or fawn' response. However, when we are not actually under attack and our lives are not at risk, it's usually counterproductive.

This reflection helped me to develop a question. Instead of meeting criticism with robust defence, questioning the evidence and others' perceptions of reality, rebutting with mountains of evidence to the contrary, proving that we're right and the feedback was wrong: what if we asked ourselves: 'If this were true, what would we do differently?'

Part of the reason for the structure of this question, starting with 'If this were true', is that it bypasses any discussion about whether or not we agree with the feedback. We are not in that moment accepting the truth and beating ourselves up with it. Nor are we denying any truth in the feedback and railing against it. Instead, we explore what we could change about ourselves, our leadership, and our decisions if the feedback were true. What gems might we find in that exploration that might help us to grow and become better leaders?

I shared this with the leadership team at Newcastle, to try to encourage us to suspend our judgement on the value and validity of the criticism and to consider what and how we might change if it were true. The impact, if I'm honest, was mixed. Some were ready to hear and consider that concept; others were not. This may have been dependent on the extent to which they were involved, and the level of hurt they were experiencing. Some may have found the challenge to their beliefs about the world in which they operated, and their behaviours and actions within that, too great to consider.

It's fair to say that many of us have been taught to weigh up the validity of the criticism before reacting – indeed, that's what I advocate when dealing with imposter phenomenon. After all, if a leader responded to everyone who wasn't happy with something they had done, they would become ineffective as a leader, oscillating between one course of action and another. However, feedback sometimes comes from more than one person's perspective, as was the case with the CQC feedback, or repeatedly, which means that it bears some further consideration and a suspension of judgement. Sometimes, feedback will come from someone who holds significant influence over others, their perceptions and behaviours. It is always worth applying the 'if this were true' question to this, as it helps to give a view of what change could be possible while removing any undue bias given to a more authoritative voice.

This applies when you receive personal feedback, too. Not too long ago, I received feedback about how an individual perceived me and my leadership style, along with their perceptions of other leaders. It was tough to hear for many reasons. We like to think of ourselves as being the best kind of person, driven by the right motives and following the right purpose. We like to think that people generally think well of us, and positive feedback from those we encounter nourishes and encourages that self-belief. That was certainly the position I'd been in over recent years. My self-confidence has grown significantly since I stopped allowing imposter phenomenon to influence me, and feedback from colleagues and others made me believe I was doing the right things in the right way. However, the feedback I received on this occasion did more than just challenge that. It completely rocked my sense of self. It described a person far from the way I saw myself, and I was devastated that anyone experienced me in that way, let alone someone who claimed to be speaking on behalf of others.

The easiest option for me would have been to go into 'fight or flight' mode, but my earlier experience, as well as the process I'd gone through to counter imposter phenomenon, gave me a couple of other options. So:

- I shared the gist of what had been said, and asked others who worked closely with me, and whose opinions I valued, for honest and clear feedback. I made it very clear that honesty was more important than my feelings: if this was the way I behaved, I needed to know and to change it (seeking evidence/counter evidence).

- I asked myself and others: 'If this were true, what would I do differently?'

I'm relieved to say that when I sought honest feedback from a wider group of people, it confirmed that these people did not share the negative opinion that had been shared with me.

Asking 'if this were true' resulted in a number of observations and potential actions that could improve the situation if the feedback was true. When you have some potential actions, as was the case in this situation, this is when it's important to ask a second, follow-up question: 'Why can't I do that anyway?'

So I considered possible actions and asked myself what would be the cost – in effort, possible adverse reactions, and financial outlay – of just doing the actions anyway.

- Could taking all, or some, of these actions improve things, even if the feedback was inaccurate, because there is always room for improvement?

- Would the input required to take the actions outweigh the benefits of taking them? If not, why not just do it?

This was an extremely useful process to go through. Once it was complete, we added it to our bag of leadership tools and I think it has helped the team become better, more reflective, leaders as a result.

Growth mindset or ubuntu?

Since then, I've done some thinking about where this approach might sit, both within accepted leadership theory and in wider world view-concepts and philosophies. You might ask, why didn't I just go to leadership theory? After all, it is well researched, has many years of application and feedback, and is collectively accepted as a sound basis for any leadership practice. However, it is not the only way, and I increasingly feel that my leadership style is not solely the result of my Western upbringing and exposure to accepted Western leadership methods. My Ashanti–Geordie roots have been seasoned by my marriage into South Asian culture and garnished by my interest in cultures and practices around the world. I strive to be authentic in all aspects of my life, including my work and professional career. So I wanted here to touch on some of those world-views and philosophies, as they may contain things that you'd like to draw on too. And if it were true what would you do differently?

Growth mindset: This term was coined by Carol Dweck. If we have a growth mindset, we believe our abilities can develop and improve through effort, learning, and persistence. Seeing feedback as an opportunity for growth and learning rather than as a threat to our self-worth or our competence allows us to grow as individuals and leaders.

Ubuntu: This comes from the Bantu African people and is often described by the phrase 'I am because we are'. It talks of our interconnectedness and the importance of our collective wellbeing. When we ask 'If this were true, what would we do differently?', we are attempting to see things from other perspectives to support collective growth and learning. This also needs leaders to have a degree of humility and to accept that our personal and professional growth is linked to receiving feedback and input from others.

Adaptive leadership theory: Developed by Ronald Heifetz and Marty Linsky, this is a leadership model that welcomes change. Adaptive leaders embrace learning and continuous growth, are able to change what they're doing when something isn't working, and welcome feedback and the diverse and unique perspectives different people can bring. When we look for potential truths in feedback and then examine what we could do differently to address these, we show that we're willing to take feedback constructively and to use it to improve our effectiveness as leaders.

First Nations leadership: This refers to the leadership concepts of the people of North America who inhabited the land before it was colonised by Europeans. Leadership within First Nations peoples is seen as a duty and responsibility to the community. The emphasis is on humility, listening, and adaptability. When we put aside judgement about feedback we have received in favour of looking at how we can change to address it, we show that we are able to self-reflect and listen to multiple perspectives to shape our leadership styles and better serve our organisation.

The ladder of inference: This was developed by Chris Argyris and Donald Schoen, and is often used to help people remain objective and avoid unnecessary mistakes. It describes how we tend to jump to conclusions based on our assumptions and beliefs. When we ask, 'If this were true...' we are immediately challenging our assumptions, putting them to one side to allow us to consider alternative options and perspectives before making a decision or taking action.

Te Ao Māori: Coming from the Māori people of New Zealand, this world-view emphasises our interconnectedness, respect for others, and the need for continuous improvement through learning. Leaders are expected to learn by seeking and receiving feedback on an ongoing basis. A willingness to listen to feedback, even when it is challenging or difficult to accept, and to examine what could be done differently, aligns with this perspective and approach.

Yorùbá leadership philosophy: Coming from the Yorùbá people of West Africa, this leadership philosophy emphasises a balance of wisdom, humility, and responsiveness to the needs of, and feedback from, the community. Our willingness to look for potential truth in the feedback we receive and to refine and develop ourselves and our leadership style through self-reflection and the input of others is strongly aligned with seeking to be what the Yorùbá call Ọmọlúàbí (a person of good character), something I believe all leaders should be.

So, there are a number of bases for taking this approach in accepted leadership and world-view theory. What I love about these world-view theories is their sense of collectivism and collaboration, as well as the idea that a leader has a responsibility to the people they lead. However, as I mentioned above, asking, 'if this were true' won't always be appropriate, but it is worth considering, especially when every fibre screams at you to ignore it.

To finish this chapter, I'd like to emphasise that, just because you are considering the possibility that feedback may be true, this does not mean that it is. Considering feedback is a useful way to allow you to explore possibilities for change and improvement, rather than miss a learning opportunity because you don't like the way it is packaged.

Key Learning Points

Reflect on Feedback Without Judgment: Asking 'If this were true, what would I do differently?' allows leaders to step away from defensiveness and explore potential improvements without committing to the accuracy of the feedback.

Explore Without Agreement: This method enables constructive consideration of feedback, even when it challenges your self-perception, instead of dismissing it outright.

Separate Emotion from Action: Instead of reacting emotionally to feedback, using this approach creates space for rational reflection and potential growth.

Engage Others for Perspective: Seeking feedback from trusted colleagues can provide clarity on whether criticism is reflective of broader perspectives or isolated opinions.

Consider Proactive Improvements: Even if feedback isn't entirely accurate, exploring and implementing beneficial changes can lead to growth and improved outcomes.

Adaptability as Strength: Leaders benefit from a willingness to reframe challenges and criticism as opportunities for learning and growth, demonstrating humility and resilience.

Connect Leadership with Community Wellbeing: Approaches like ubuntu, Te Ao Māori, and Yorùbá leadership philosophies remind leaders of their interconnectedness and responsibility to their teams.

Balance Feedback with Evidence: While considering feedback, leaders should weigh it against collective input and evidence to make balanced, thoughtful decisions.

If you want to learn more take a look at:

Growth mindset: Carol Dweck's *Mindset: The New Psychology of Success. (Book)*

Ubuntu philosophy: Priscilla Mtungwa Ndlovu's *Discovering the Spirit of Ubuntu Leadership* (Book)

Desmond Tutu's *No Future Without Forgiveness. (Book)*

First Nations leadership: Robin Wall Kimmerer's 'Braiding Sweetgrass'. (Book)

Ladder of Inference: Developed by Chris Argyris and Donald Schoen, this theory helps leaders challenge assumptions and avoid premature conclusions.

Te Ao Māori world view: Articles on Māori leadership in The Journal of Indigenous Wellbeing (open access).

Yorùbá leadership philosophy: In particular, Ọmọlúàbí (person of good character).

Chapter Ten

The Secret Lesson

The one where I rediscover my authentic self, embracing my individuality, confidence, and joy by breaking free from conformity.

I'm excited to share my final leadership lesson with you. It's the most fun lesson of all and it was right in front of me while I was going through many years of struggle, masking, and effort. I didn't recognise it at the time, but it was there waiting patiently for me. All I had to do was notice it and embrace it. It's a lesson that, as the make-up experts say, is buildable, so you can get as much coverage as you want. But the key thing is that it is also very individual. What is right for me in this lesson won't be right for you, so do what you feel suits you best and play with it.

There's a picture of me as a child that I love. I'm standing in my granda's back garden and I'm wearing a snazzy pair of red and yellow trousers – proper bobby-dazzlers, as we say in the north-east. My naturally curly hair is pulled up into a very messy bun (I suspect it was a lot tidier at the start of the day) and I'm standing at an angle but looking straight at the camera with a cheeky little smile, my hands clasped in front of me, looking for all the world like I'm about to give a talk or issue instructions. The picture was taken around the time of my second birthday. By all accounts I was a boisterous, enthusiastic, curious child: confident, happy, and full of life.

I have another picture of me, taken when I was assistant director of operations at North East Ambulance Service. I must be about thirty-six. I have straight hair, I'm wearing no make-up or jewellery, and I'm overweight. What is more, although this might not be visible to most people, I can see a whole lot of sadness in my eyes. It shows the version of me that felt like I didn't fit in, that was allowing imposter phenomenon to rule me. It's the version of me that worked ridiculously long hours in the hope I'd make myself useful by doing a lot, even if I didn't do it particularly well. I was desperately trying to fit into an environment where everyone was very different to me, and that meant dressing and trying to behave against my character.

Let me explain.

I was fortunate to be a participant on a number of leadership programmes during the first part of my career – the NHS Graduate Management Training Scheme, the Breaking Through Programme, and the Breaking Through Top Talent Programme. One of the things we were taught was that the way you dressed influenced your career progression. The concept of dressing for the job you want, not the job you have, is still very common, and an internet search will show a plethora of articles telling you how to do just that. However, I believe that some of these programmes, particularly those for ethnically minoritised managers, wanted to help managers appear part of the establishment through our clothing choices and behaviours. I understand that much of this was about self-preservation: we were going to stand out just by having brown skin in a middle/senior leadership role, so it could be advisable to make sure that we wore the NHS management 'uniform', so there wasn't another reason to single us out. I was given an interview tip: to make myself look as much like someone who already worked for the organisation, at the level I wanted to work, as I could. This included suggestions like taking a folder in with me rather than a handbag, and looking at what the people in senior roles within the organisation wore and emulating that.

The role I applied for, and subsequently got, at the ambulance service reported directly to the executive directors. When I checked out the Board, the executives were all white men in their forties and fifties, predominantly grey-haired and grey-suited with white shirts. Well, it was going to be a challenge to make myself look like them. But I tried. I didn't wear any make-up, wore a small pair of earrings, tied my hair up, and wore a dark trouser suit with a white shirt. My version of the grey man. I don't know if it helped my interview but it certainly can't have hurt, as I got the job.

What followed was years of me trying to wear the uniform. At the ambulance service it was mainly trouser suits; when I wore a skirt one day, I got a comment about the fact I had legs, and I stopped wearing certain tops because of comments about my cleavage. When I moved from there to the North of Tyne Primary Care Trust, I continued to wear a lot of trouser suits. It wasn't until I joined the clinical commissioning group and we had a female chief operating officer who always wore tailored dresses that I branched out and started to wear dresses and skirts (all tailored and mainly in sombre colours).

The way I dressed was a reflection of the way I behaved. I tried to behave the way I believed a leader should: to be professional. To my mind, this meant not just dressing the part but also:

- Being serious, not flippant or overly casual with colleagues
- Making sure I had the answers – all the answers
- Making sure I didn't make mistakes – or, if I did, that I fixed them before anyone noticed
- Trying to blend in and not stand out (that old chestnut again)
- Being emotionally bland – no high or low moods
- Making sure I was always busy (remember the busy-ness myth).

I put on that uniform and play-acted being a manager and a leader. Colleagues might say I wasn't very good at play-acting. I find it hard to act out of character, but I put real effort into it and the costume was always on point.

Let's go back to the two photos of me. When I look at those two photos, it's like the difference between Kansas and Oz. One is bright and colourful and full of joy and the other is black, white, and grey – and, for me at least, tinged with sadness.

What happened to two-year-old Steph? Well, life happened. If you've read all this book, you'll know that experience fed the imposter phenomenon and I allowed it to influence my thinking and my choices. I wasn't kind to myself, I chose to hide who I was, and I prioritised everyone and everything over me. People saw me, but not the whole of me; to paraphrase The Waterboys, they saw the crescent and not the whole of the moon.

I've talked about the steps I took to ensure imposter phenomenon was not a dominating factor in my life and all the little life lessons I learned along the way, but this last lesson is about recapturing that part of me that had been buried and left long ago.

When I created the café I mentioned in Chapter 5, I worked with two junior management trainees. One, Sarah, was full of life and ambition. She had left the NHS after a few years and worked abroad before returning to the UK and setting up a nail salon. We'd connected on Facebook and I'd seen all of this unfold, often saying I'd pop in to get my nails done sometime. A few weeks after a trip to Ghana, I bumped into her in a petrol station. I'd had acrylic nails done when in Ghana and they'd left my natural nails in a shocking state, so I finally decided to visit her and have my nails painted with gel polish. Over the following six or seven years I have invested time and money in myself and visited Sarah's salon every few weeks (Covid lockdowns allowing). I looked forward to our catch-ups and chats, and my chance to do something just for me. At first, I chose very neutral colours for my nails, nothing too eye-catching, but this gradually changed and I started to experiment with colour. Could I get away with bright green? What about neon orange? What about Christmas bauble nail art? Could I break the rules, just a little bit? Could I be a little bit naughty?

Once I'd started on my journey to reclaim myself, I felt that my nails weren't enough. I recall walking across the car park on the way to work and thinking about how I was never going to fit in; I would always stand out. I can remember thinking: 'I am going to stand out no matter what I do, but if I stand out, then I am outstanding!'

If I was going to be outstanding, then it was going to be in the way I wanted to be – I was going to be a little bit naughtier. I started to wear colour, and I mean the bright, bold colours I love. Block colour dresses in citrus orange, cobalt blue, emerald green, and, yes the most forbidden colour of all (because it's aggressive, apparently) – red!

Bold colours suit me, and colour is part of my cultural identity. Kente cloth, generally seen by the world as the African cloth, originated from Bonwire in the Ashanti region of Ghana, where men weave it in brightly coloured and intricately patterned strips on wooden looms. Not wearing bright colours meant muting myself and my identity to fit in with the norms of a society and a system that I didn't fit in with, and what is more I realised I don't need to fit in with it: I need to stand out. Be outstanding. So today I choose to be naughty and I wear the bold colours I love.

Earlier in this chapter I described the professional persona I believed I had to adopt as a uniform. A uniform is something that makes you appear to be part of the organisation you belong to. As a Guider, I take pride in wearing my uniform and being identified as part of the world's largest organisation for girls and women. But the professional uniform I wore for work, trying my best to fit in, didn't give me that sense of belonging and pride. It was itchy and ill-fitting. I felt like it was a costume, something I was wearing to transform myself into something I wasn't. It was a dress-up box imitation of the thing I thought I should be. Since I've become a little bit naughty, my clothing is now a part of me and an expression of me, not a barrier, uniform, or costume.

Now, I'm not telling you that you have to wear bright green and have sparkly nails. That's my thing. It's what makes me confident, happy, and full of life. Your thing might be, and probably is, something different.

I gave a talk at a girls' school speech day recently and one of the mothers mentioned to me afterwards that she had an awards dinner coming up but that she didn't like to wear colour; she preferred monochrome. She also hated wearing dresses, but women are expected to wear an evening dress at these type of events. I told her that her version of naughty was to wear the trousers. So she did. And she looked magnificent!

But being yourself isn't just about appearance. My little acts of rebellion, the small ways in which I reclaimed myself, gave me the confidence to portray more of myself at work. I started to relax the professional persona I'd put so much effort into maintaining and allowed myself to be myself at work. I laughed more – and never more than in my current role at St Oswald's Hospice. I shared more about who I was, what motivated me, and how I worked best. I kept on finding ways to be a little bit naughty, challenging perceived wisdom and the status quo, and I encouraged others to break the rules.

During the first few months of the pandemic, which was when I started as CEO at St Oswald's Hospice, I realised we needed to do things differently if we were to thrive, not just survive. I told people that now was the time to start doing new and different things, or the same things in new and different ways, as long as they were 'safe, legal, and wouldn't break the bank'. It was a bit playful but I wanted people to know they could experiment and try new things. That they had my encouragement and permission, if it was needed, to break the rules and to innovate. If things worked, then that was great, and we could learn from that. If things didn't work, then that would be good too, because we could also learn from that. Because that's what rule breakers do: they innovate and stimulate innovation in others.

When everyone is the same, doing the same thing, forcing themselves into the same mould, that rarely fits comfortably, we constrain ourselves and our imaginations; we limit our creativity and drain ourselves of energy. Being a little bit naughty not only allows us to be the individuals that we are; it also allows us to be outstanding in our own way – at work and in life.

Being a little bit naughty is safe; it's not about walking up to the boss, telling them exactly what you think of them and their leadership style and storming out of the office, sweeping papers off desks on your way (or whatever the virtual version of that would be). It's about taking small steps, testing the ground, and feeling your way into being authentic in your life, including when you're at work. For me, breaking the rules is often about breaking those unwritten rules, about challenging 'how things are done around here' and shaking up the status quo.

Being a little bit naughty is fun: it's about being playful and curious, testing out how doing something you enjoy, something that is true to you, feels in a different environment, and what happens as a result (I'm fairly certain the sky won't fall in).

Being a little bit naughty is what has allowed me to be that two-year-old in the photo again – boisterous, enthusiastic, curious, confident, happy, and full of life. 'Be a little bit naughty' is my final leadership lesson for you, and I hope it brings you joy!

'If you're always trying to be normal, you will never know how amazing you can be.' ***Maya Angelou***

Key Learning Points

Authenticity is Empowering: Embrace your true self in both appearance and behaviour, rather than conforming to a standard or "uniform" that doesn't fit your identity or values.

Small Acts of Rebellion Can Be Transformative: Taking small steps to challenge norms and express individuality, like wearing bold colours or breaking unwritten rules, can lead to greater confidence and authenticity.

Leadership and Authenticity Go Hand in Hand: Allowing yourself to be genuine at work by sharing who you are, encouraging laughter, and fostering openness, creates an environment where others can thrive too.

Creativity Thrives on Breaking Rules: Innovation often stems from challenging established practices or norms. Experimentation, even if it involves failure, can lead to learning and growth.

Confidence Comes From Being True to Yourself: Reclaiming elements of your personality and finding joy in them can reignite energy and positivity in your personal and professional life.

Leadership Is About Encouraging Others: Provide your team with the freedom and support to experiment, innovate, and find their own ways to excel.
Joy and Playfulness Have a Place in Leadership: Leadership doesn't always have to be serious; being playful and embracing small joys can create a vibrant, motivated, and collaborative workplace.

If you want to learn more take a look at:

Growth Mindset: Brené Brown's *The Power of Vulnerability*. (Book)

Carol Dweck's *Mindset: The New Psychology of Success*. (Book)

Simon Sinek's *Start With Why*. (Book)

Francesca Gino's *Rebel Talent*. (Book)

W. Chan Kim and Renée Mauborgne's *Blue Ocean Strategy*. (Book)

Ubuntu philosophy: Priscilla Mtungwa Ndlovu's *Discovering the Spirit of Ubuntu Leadership* (Book)

Desmond Tutu's *No Future Without Forgiveness. (Book)*

Te Ao Māori world view: Articles on Māori leadership in The Journal of Indigenous Wellbeing (open access).

Acknowledgements

To my family – especially my daughter, Yasmin, and my partner, Rob – I offer my deepest gratitude for their patience and understanding as I poured my focus into this book. Their tolerance of my long hours, occasional distractions, even rare tantrums, and their unwavering support has been invaluable, not just throughout this project but in all my endeavours.

To Risaria Langley, the most encouraging, challenging, loving, and joyful writing coach – I am endlessly grateful for your guidance and belief in me.

To Claire Bennett, Claudia Venosa-Hepworth, James Carss, Ngozi Lyn Cole, Ranjana Bell, Sheinaz Stansfield, Sophie World, and Steph Whitehead – thank you for your generosity in sharing your time, expertise, and insights. Your invaluable feedback has helped shape this book into something that I hope will resonate with leaders at all stages of their careers.

Finally, to everyone who has expressed genuine interest and enthusiasm for this book, whether in person or online, thank you. I hope it meets (and even exceeds) your expectations.

About the Author

Steph Edusei is the Chief Executive of St Oswald's Hospice, a large children and adults charitable hospice. She's also a Director of the North East Chamber of Commerce, Chair of Tyneside Cinema, and a member of the Chartered Management Institute's Women's Committee.

As an integral part of her local community, Steph has been a leader with Girlguiding UK for over 30 years and holds the position of Chair at Eliot Smith Dance Company. Previously, she served as a Non-Executive Director of The Newcastle upon Tyne Hospitals NHS Foundation Trust and was the co-chair of The Angelou Centre, a charity offering training, counselling, and refuge support.

Steph is the founder and host of the 'Black All Year' podcast and associated events. She uses the platform to amplify Black voices, highlight the challenges faced by Black people, and celebrate their successes and achievements.

In 2022, Steph was named Transformational Leader at the Northern Power Women Awards and was included on the Northern Power Women Power List in 2025, recognising those who are shifting the dial towards a more gender equal world.

Additionally, in 2024, she was featured on the prestigious Business Cloud Northern Leaders List.

Connect with Steph's LinkedIn: www.linkedin.com/in/steph-edusei

Listen to the 'Black All Year' podcast: www.blackallyear.co.uk

Printed in Dunstable, United Kingdom

63788140R00080